5000 YEARS BACK

A TIMELESS CONVERSATION

NEETIKA MAHESHWARI KASAT

Copyright © Neetika Maheshwari Kasat
All Rights Reserved.

This book has been published with all efforts taken to make the material error-free after the consent of the author. However, the author and the publisher do not assume and hereby disclaim any liability to any party for any loss, damage, or disruption caused by errors or omissions, whether such errors or omissions result from negligence, accident, or any other cause.

While every effort has been made to avoid any mistake or omission, this publication is being sold on the condition and understanding that neither the author nor the publishers or printers would be liable in any manner to any person by reason of any mistake or omission in this publication or for any action taken or omitted to be taken or advice rendered or accepted on the basis of this work. For any defect in printing or binding the publishers will be liable only to replace the defective copy by another copy of this work then available.

To my grandmother, Respected Smt Rameshwari Devi
Kasat, whom I have always seen reading Holy Gita every
day, through out her life, without fail and with
unshakable devotion for Lord Krishna. Every day she
reads with the kind of dedication as if she is reading for
the first time and its been continuing for last 90 years.
Every moment spent with her, every conversation with
her, had inspired me to the core and will continue to
touch our lives, forever....

To my parents - Respected Urmila and Pradeep
Maheshwari, who are my heros and who supported
unflinchingly even after knowing I may come up with
something bizarre. Not sure what these parents species
are made up of. Thank you for always showering your love
and blessings on us.

Last but first- everything I do, belongs to Absolute
Supreme Authority Sri Radha-Krishna and to our beloved
Guru as without their blessings, nothing would fall in
place.

Contents

Contents

सुखदुःखे समे कृत्वा लाभालाभौ जयाजयौ ।
ततो युद्धाय युज्यस्व नैवं पापमवाप्स्यसि ॥

Fight for the sake of duty, treating alike happiness and distress, loss and gain, victory and defeat. Fulfilling your responsibilities in this way, you will never incur sin.

When Adi Sankara wanted to convey his Vedanta to his disciples, he simply went to the Mahabharata and recited a commentary on Bhagwad Gita . The learned Sankara had the wisdom to know that to get high philosophy across, one needs to have a strong base in reality. The Bhagwad Gita was seen as carrying the very essence of life experience, clarity of what is right and what is wrong, the varied colours of human nature, and the subtle pathways of Dharma.

The other day I was asking a friend's 15 year old if he knew about Mahabharata. And he said no! Now partly it was because I chose the wrong time to ask i.e. when he was playing a game. But I was still taken aback as she had read him stories about Mahabharata when he was younger, Told him about anecdotes on some occasions and he has been exposed to scriptures as much as was possible. That got me thinking about how to bring back those learnings and stories which were perhaps stored deep down in his sub conscious mind. He is not the only one I am sure. But now the challenge was that he is past the age of the story books as they were more geared towards toddlers and he is still not at the adulthood stage where he can pick up the scripture and read it. That's the gap this book is attempting to plug.

Neetika is a qualified and well established chartered accountant/entrepreneur running a very successful business. My association with Neetika began 22 years ago when she had just started out on the professional journey. Even then she was always inclined towards spirituality and meaning of life. She had the desire to understand and was seeking the deeper meaning of life through the scriptures. Bhagwad Gita was the most sacred powerhouse of life lessons that we used to discuss about. Questions such as, what is the gist of Gita? How can we better understand it and use those learnings in our daily lives and many such questions and curiosities of a young mind. Over the years life took over and we got busy with responsibilities. As her son was growing up, she wanted to impart that knowledge over to him. That's when the idea of this book was conceptualised. This is a brilliant attempt to give practical lessons through scriptures using a modern-day context which is more relatable to the younger generation.

The tale unfolds through 18 chapters taking you on an exciting journey of learning about different characters of Mahabharata with discussion points and illustrations. This book will challenge you to think and reflect. Neetika has succinctly captured the essence of Gita through an approach that will resonate with the young minds who are regularly exposed to the world of super heroes and simulated battlefields and technological advancement. Hope you enjoy this book as much as I did.

Radhika Patwardhan Ghanekar

Trustee, UTSAAH Initiative, UK registered Charity dedicated to work wtih remote villages in Himalayas

Chartered Certified Accountant, UK

Acknowledgements

Gratitude word is not enough to describe all the efforts that my sister Kanika Maheshwari has put in. She is the supporting pillar of my life and has shaped up the book beautifully by giving wonderful ideas. Many thanks dear sister. My life is incomplete without you and thanks for laying the foundation for this book.

My closest and loving friend , Radhika Patwardhan Ghanekar, whose first reaction to this idea was a raised eyebrow and a loud laughter but insisted me to go on, even if its the most stupid idea on the earth. Her detailed review for weeks, valuable suggestions, ever lasting encouragement have all led the book to be a reality. Dear Radha, it would not have been possible without your presence. Many thanks for writing foreword for the book.

My teenager son , Samatva N Kasat , who was frank enough to call my book as "boring" and when I said fine, lets drop the idea, he jumped around and said "dont stop Mamma", sometimes "most boring stuff can turn out to be cool"- you never know! Thank you my son and thank you for being the editor.

My in-laws, Respected Pushpa and Gopal Kasat who have always supported me in my journey, which is full of new ventures. Their love and blessings are countless.

Heartfelt thanks to my husband, Amit Kasat, who had been silently inspiring at every step and for sharing his intelligence and deep knowledge on Indian heritage, which has helped a lot with the book.

Lastly, to all my other friends and well- wishers who have sent their valuable suggestions.

Thank you all!

1

Dive into the past

A walk in woods

One cold December afternoon, five brothers were loitering in the nearby woods while enjoying the warm and soft sunrays. Pondering over their past experience, they realized they were amongst the fortunate ones as they could come out of their hardships. Their hearts were filled with gratitude for the generosity universe had bestowed upon them and gave them courage to walk on the path of truth, honesty and duty. It all started flashing back. Yudi, the most calm, balanced and eldest brother, as always, urged others to be grateful to their parents and elders in the family as without their blessings, it would have been a very difficult journey. Bobby, who always carries a bit of impulsiveness in his mind, snapped around to disagree with his brother saying that all relatives had been unfair and supported their cousins who had brutally thrown them out of the family and took over their share of wealth. Yudi, with a smile on his lips, requested his younger brother to forget all the miseries as today they are living a peaceful and comfortable life. This was a common scene and other brothers were used to the erratic behavior of their second eldest brother Bobby. They kept walking quietly but with tremendous turbulence in their minds. Nick and Dave were the youngest ones who prefer not to get into any arguments ever. Aarj- a fighter at heart, but full of compassion always, started unfolding the pages from the past. Quietly, they continued walking on the familiar trail, spotting colorful flowers on the sides, bushes loaded with berries, occasionally hearing cuckoo sound and their own steps as they walked further. With every step forward, their thoughts went back in the past. They came across a giant rock, which was their usual resting place. Warm sun rays enveloped the rock and made it shine like gold. Like always, today also they sat there, looking down the hill and that's when Aarj went deep diving into the past.

Pondering into the past

Flashback 35 years, Aarj saw himself as a 12-year-old pre-teenager boy, living a comfortable life in a palace like house with his mother, uncles, aunts, grandparents and other cousins. He remembers how they tried to have a cordial relationship with the cousins, but somehow it did not work out. On several occasions, it was apparent how their cousins were jealous of them. They were insecured as they knew that these five brothers are hard-working, perseverant, wise and blessed with a charismatic personality. Instead of being proud of their brothers, they started disliking them.

Memories from childhood

Their cousin brothers developed more hatred on every occasion where these five brothers won an award or a competition or were just praised in school by the teachers. Five brothers were quite hard working and victory mostly took their sides – not because they were influential or lucky, but because they did put their blood and sweat and never took short cuts when it came to hard work.

School days

They used to bag awards all the time, sometimes beating their cousins in the tournaments if they happened to be in the opposite teams. Be it cricket or basketball or boxing or academics, most of the time, they achieved laurels.

Yudi always tried encouraging cousins but Bobby's sometimes thoughtless whims may turn into a mockery and the cousins could not take those comments in the healthy way. This is how the rivalry started in their hearts. Bobby should also have been considerate using words and made sure words for fun do not pierce anyone's hearts. How small childhood fights turned into a bitter grudge in the hearts of cousins and before they realized, the poison of jealousy and envy had started seeping in, showing cracks in their relationships. Somehow, even in spite of various patch up efforts put in by elders, the cousins could never stop feeling vehemently towards Yudi and his brothers. It took a nasty shape when their maternal uncle along with other company management, prepared fake and illegal ownership documents. Before Yudi and his brothers realized, they were thrown off the family property.

Growing up in misery

Their father had died few years back and mother did not take enough interest in the business. At the age of 13, Aarj realized, they have no money!! They had to leave the palatial house to stay in the servant's cottage. Now cousins kept insulting them and all Bobby could do was to clench his fist and lips- nothing beyond that. He was facing the consequences of his own mischiefs which were innocent for that time but gradually watered the seeds of bitterness and now it has grown into a huge tree of contempt and avarice. How everyone wished if it was corrected right then during childhood times when the boys were like soft ball of mud and the relationship could have been molded in a better shape. Those were the fundamental years of one's character but unfortunately things went from bad to worse.

Young men now - life is still tough

Years went by- some days were good, some turned out to be more painful than others but wheel of life went on.

Boys turned into young, strong and handsome looking men. They almost turned 20 and decided to speak up for their share in the wealth. What has happened few years back was not right and they were hopeful that their uncles might give them their fair share in the family wealth.

If not full, at least some small portion so the boys could settle down, live a happy life and nurture their families. Surprisingly, when this topic was brought up, even the unbiased uncles and aunts decided to be quiet. They did not have enough courage to go against the rich and powerful. Amongst relatives, the only person who supported them was their maternal cousin brother Kris. They all grew up together, few years apart and would spend almost all summer vacations together. They had love and respect for each other. Kris always supported the idea of asking for their share, or even fight for it if needed. Brothers also approached their cousins and asked for their righteous share which was actually due to them. In return, they were insulted, shrugged off and thrown out of the office. Five brothers even were ready to settle for much smaller share than what was due to them as they just wanted to start their lives. They were confident of their ability to grow that small share into a successful large business. They did not carry high ambitions on the cost of greed.

Ray of hope - cousin Kris

Kris, a wise and a successful, rich young man himself thought of approaching the wicked cousins to see if they were willing to talk and give a reasonable share. Five brothers were even ready to let everything else go. They just need some money so they can start small businesses and live a decent life. There was nothing wrong to ask for what was rightfully theirs.

Kris was a successful, influential and accomplished business man. For this reason, it was difficult for the cousins to dismiss him immediately. They knew Kris was powerful enough to capture their business or even wipe them out completely from the business world. Thus, cousins would like to deal carefully with Kris as his support would mean a lot to them. They welcomed Kris and showered warm hospitality and tried to even lure Kris's mind by offering him more business opportunities. Of course, the main reason behind all this was to persuade Kris to stop supporting Yudi and his brothers. Kris was a man of words and ethics and no such offer could distract him from the path of righteousness. Kris played the role of a mediator and tried to convince the cousins to give a fair share to the five brothers.

Duro, eldest brother, did not like anyone who would support his five cousins. He tried to hold himself when Kris was trying to convince them. But could not put up a calm face for long. His volcano of anger erupted and started being bitter with Kris in his conversation. This is another sign of immaturity when someone could not hold a conversation in a cool way. He started blaming five brothers for their own miseries.

Discussion with Duro

Kris tried to stop Duro from being bitter but it's difficult for these kind of people whose intelligence is overshadowed by anger and jealousy. Duro went on throwing words of poison and he went to the extent of insulting Kris by asking him to leave from there. He had crossed all his limits.

Kris, always a calm, composed character walked out with heavy heart but determined mind! He knew the five brothers have to stand up and now fight for their fair share.

Duro - full of arrogance and greed

The five brothers were waiting with hope and anticipation, but, as soon as Kris stepped in, they could sense it wasn't going to be a good one.

Before Kris could say anything, Bobby busted into a fit of anger. Yudi calmed him down and asked Kris to narrate all what happened. Other brothers stood quietly with tearful eyes. Their hopes were shattered. They had immense faith that Kris could turn the table around and make it fair for everyone. But they had no idea that Duro was much swelled up with pride and false ego, he even committed a blunder of humiliating Kris!

How much they tried to solve the issues in amicable manner, how much they wanted to avoid a nasty litigation but all efforts in vain. Seems like a legal war has to happen! But how can the brothers fight legally as well, as it needs a good amount of money. Top lawyers need to get paid, frequent travels, the costs looked endless and even though Kris offered his help, Yudi humbly declined. Yudi did not want to borrow or take financial help when he did not know how to pay it back. He was ready to suffer than ask someone for help as if he loses, he would never be able to repay it. All four brothers and Kris could read his thoughts and developed more respect for him in their hearts. But respect cannot get food or shelter or the life they were looking forward to. They have to stand up and fight-question was how?

How weeks passed by and brothers went through more times of misery! Conditions change only when a step is taken. As they say, God helps those who help themselves. They again tried to approach their cousins and this time they asked for a very small share, just enough from them to earn a livelihood and live a modest life. They were okay to let go majority of the wealth. Again, they were kicked out like how people shoo away stray dogs! They kept drinking poison and went through several instances of humiliation.

What next?

Kris offered them a part of his wealth many times but every time the brothers humbly refused as their mother has always taught them not to take favors from anyone if they don't know have a plan to return it. They were willing to live in poverty but not go on the path of asking favors. They were full of self-respect and wanted to earn it for themselves or live with what is rightfully deserved!

There is an end to everything, even to hopelessness! Kris came up with an idea of organizing a boxing championship in the town.

A very unique kind of championship where the loser does not just lose the title but also his money and boxing career! News spread like fire as everyone knew Kris will be coaching one of the best boxer of the time – Aarj! Aarj started practicing day and night, having full focus on the championship, knowing that winning this could be a table turner. It can actually end their miseries as winning this title would mean lot of respect, name, fame and riches may follow. They may be able to win it all. Although the wealth belongs to the entire family but now Aarj has to put in more efforts to win it back from Duro. Giving up does not help. Sometimes, we do need to fight in order to bring justice.

They knew Duro could not resist participating and rather it was a challenge for him. He was an impulsive, short tempered and egoistic person. The message was conveyed to him and it was insulting for a boxer to refuse the fight for the fear of losing it. It is not befitting Duro. So, he agreed and in his swollen pride, he also impulsively declared that if the final fight happens between Aarj and Duro, the loser will give up all the wealth and will move out of the city. Well, the loser can also die as the rules of the final game were different! Not just different, but dangerous too!

But as suspected by Kris, Duro went furious and he started condemning this event which was planned for the next year. He knew Aarj is one of the best boxers and it won't be surprising if he wins the title. Duro was himself a very trained and strong boxer, who had won numerous games but still he was not sure if he could stand against Aarj. He knew Kris himself is coaching Aarj and more than anything it's the coach that really matters the most. Duro knew that Kris was a man of words and full of honesty and ethics. He approached Kris and asked him bitterly- How come you are so biased to Aarj and not to me? I also have a right to take you as my coach and if you claim to be so fair, there is no reason for you to reject me. Kris smiled and said certainly. He was reading Duro's mind and he knew how to lure him while being fair at the same time. He threw a bait. He told Duro that he was planning to spend a big amount of money on Aarj's training – get him the best gloves, accessories, mentors from different part of the world and everything that it needs for him to prepare. If any money remains, it would still go to Aarj.

Duro eyes started rolling! Kris threw his next bait – He offered Duro same amount of money. He gave him a choice of either taking money or take Kris as the coach. If Duro chooses Kris as his coach, then the money goes to Aarj which can be used for world class training and other expenses. On the other hand, if Duro chooses money over Kris's mentorship then Kris is free to be a coach for Aarj. Depending upon what Duro chooses, Aarj will have to settle with the other choice.

Duro snapped back asking what kind of arrangement is this? Kris replied saying this is the fairest arrangement and if Duro is not happy with it then he can withdraw his name from the championship and let Aarj be the World Title Winner. This could never be acceptable to Duro as he was full of envy and greed. He could not see anything good happening with Aarj and at the same time he could not ignore the few million $ offer. Kris went a step further and said he wants to be fair to both Duro and Aarj but since Duro has an issue, he would like to make the first offer to Duro and whatever he lets go, will inturn go to Aarj. This was being more than fair to Duro. Duro stood perplexed

– letting that kind of money go was so foolish to him but he also wanted Kris as his personal coach. Kris gave him a week's time to think. Duro walked away quietly, confused on what to take and what to leave.

News reached Aarj and he went running to Kris. He put his hands-on Kris's shoulders and shook him, asking hysterically, if what he had heard is true? Kris, an always truthful man, said calmly that yes it was true. It was true that Duro has been given a choice to either choose Kris or money. Aarj cannot make that choice as the first preference is given to Duro. Aarj needs to wait for a week to accept what was rejected by Duro! Aarj eyes were filled with tears and he begged Kris to not leave him. He kept weeping hysterically and kept saying – Do I really need to make a choice? Is this first time you have offered me your wealth? I don't need it, I just need you as my coach, as my mentor and as my friend! You are our energy and please don't leave us. Kris smiled and lovingly asked Aarj not to worry. Kris was very sure that Duro, a mean, greedy and selfish man, cannot resist that kind of wealth and then Kris will be free to take side of five brothers. But they had to wait for a week and it seemed like a never-ending week, seemed like an eternity. Brothers were full of nervousness- lot of 'what's' and 'ifs' were on their mind.

Finally, the week got over and it was time for a conference. Everyone assembled at the given venue, given time. Aarj was precipitating, Yudi sat with no expressions, Bobby with his fist clenched, Nick and Dave stood quietly staring at the table. Duro and his team entered laughing loudly and making derogatory remarks on the five brothers. Bobby, the strongest brother, desperately wanted to give a reply to every comment Duro made but Yudi stopped him by giving an eye expression. Such was the kind of connection between these brothers. The entire family including elders, youngster sat together waiting for Kris to open the discussion. Everyone loved Kris but a few, loved riches more and this is what Kris was hoping for. In a fraction of moment, destiny was to be written for all of them. As promised, Duro was given the first chance to speak up his choice. With all hypocrisy, Duro bragged how much he wanted Kris to support them and to be a part of his team. Every word was making a thunderous blow in the heart of the five brothers. All they wanted Kris on their side. Duro went to Kris and asked if he would give his wishes to his team. Without a second thought, Kris replied saying his best wishes are with everyone in the room. Hearing this, Duro laughed loudly and said then this is easiest choice he probably is making in this life time. He covered for himself saying that Kris best wishes are anyways with him and why would he be foolish enough to let the money go to five brothers. He hated them and he did not want to see them living an affluent life. Duro declared that he would want to have the immense wealth Kris offered. Kris smiled from the corner of his lip and looked at Aarj. Tears started rolling on Aarj's cheeks and all five brothers hugged Kris and thanked their stars. They were filled with gratitude and quietly they walked out of the room and Kris accompanied them. So now there was a team of six who needed to work hard for the upcoming competition, a competition that could have a fatal ending.

Boxing Chamionship idea

Now a year is available for the brothers to get ready, precisely 11 months and 17 days. The 5 brothers and Kris were walking out of the room with hundreds of thoughts, plans, and questions in mind. This competition could not be taken lightly. Losing it, would mean spending the rest of their lives in rags and winning would give them lots of fame, name, and share in the family wealth and a life-long reputation in the world of boxing. Resources were limited, no proper ring to practice, no equipment for training and no option to go back. Aarj knew in his heart that this game may be the last game of his life as he may suffer permanent injuries or may even die. Duro could be very cruel and beastly. He can break the rules to his advantage. And on top of that he indeed had been a good boxer. Games should be played among equal opponents and that's when both the winner and loser get respect. The plan has to be made, schedule needs to be chalked out, diet needs to be special and 12-14 hours of training/practice every day would be the least that was required. There was no time left to even fall sick. He had to cut down on all his favorite food and just focus on healthy meal. Controlling tongue is the most difficult austerity. Kris, also a pro in boxing, has to play the role of an excellent coach. Aarj needs to turn into the most dedicated and hard-working student.

Preparations started – old and heavy tires, iron chains, 100 kg piece of log, ropes, various rocks to be used as weights, sticks, pulley to tie the rope and do weightlifting. Right from running 20 kilometers every day sometimes bare foot, sometimes with weights tied on the back or foot, punching practice and many more strenuous exercises was draining Aarj out every day. Yudi and Bobby took charge of the kitchen and made sure healthy food was available for Aarj all the time even if they need to retire hungry at night. It's a sacrifice for a year but it was needed terribly. This was the only ray of hope they had in their mind. Weeks and months passed by and now Aarj started doing better under Kris's guidance. There were boxing games held every day, Aarj was getting ready, getting better with each passing day. On the other hand, Duro, did not ever take Aarj lightly. He was equally committed and did his practice at the most sophisticated place with all modern equipment, gadgets, expensive coaches and best of the chefs. Both of them put in lot of hard work and sweat! Aarj would soon turn 22 now, but more mature for his age and more focused on his goals, he was very different from other youths. Nothing could distract him as he knew his fate and his brothers' fates depended on him.

No short cut to hard work

The tiring and gruesome training Aarg went on for almost a year. Each day in itself seemed like a year but they had to live those times too in order to get something better in future. Sometimes it's better to accept your fate without complaining, and keep working on the plan with the hope that one day things will change for good. Aarj would get 30 min of personal time during evenings and before dinner. He would sit on the same rock, near the bank of the river and just keep staring at the continuous movement of the water, the chirping of the birds which were eager to return home, the sun, ready to set. Slowly he would also look forward to a deep sleep. It was quite easy to fall asleep after a hard day of physical training. Seasons changed but this year it seemed like everything was moving too slowly. It seemed like there was only one thought in the minds of all six of them. They were functioning like one mind with six bodies. Six pair of limbs ruled by one mind. Controlling the mind is one of the most difficult tasks in the world but when the goals are clear and there is determination in your heart, your mind automatically walks on the desired path with no distractions. It's not like they did not have disturbances. Duro and his friends kept creating problems for them. Sometimes their practice place was messed up in the middle of the night, practice equipment went missing, punch bag was punctured and many more kind of troubles. The brothers did not have enough money to get them fixed.

Giving up not an option- start again

These instances would agitate them but Kris kept telling them how important is to spend energy only on fruitful activities. Energy and time is limited – one can spend time in anger, cribbing and complaining or one can understand, ignore and keep working on the goals while being more conscious and aware. People should remember their time on this planet is limited – the choice is ours on how to spend our time. Staying calm and without an ego was one of the biggest virtues that Yudi carried always and he always inspired his younger brothers but it does not come in an easy way to everyone. Yudi was born with those qualities but Bobby was a bit on the other extreme. Nevertheless, Bobby tried his best to listen to his elder brother even though it went against his characteristics.

Time passed by and before they realized, they were just four and a half months away from the competition. Seasons came and went by, festivals came, crops were harvested but it was just like another day for Aarj and his brothers. Kris was constantly with Aarj, coaching and guiding him and Aarj moved on with unalloyed faith in Kris. Training got more and more intense, more practice games, more time in the ring and less and less of other worldly task.

As the days got nearer, the excitement in the town increased. The city was lit up with different hoardings, hotels were getting booked as many people from other cities and even states would want to spectate the event, which could be just enough of its kind in this life time. Almost two hundred boxers visited from various parts of the country. Schedules were getting prepared but everyone knew that finals were really meant for Aarj- he had no choice but to win it or spend rest of the life like a rotten flesh and be a subject of mockery! A lot was at on stake, in fact, their whole lives were dependent on the outcome of this event.

Long gruelling hours

Finally, it was the night before the week-long event. The brothers ate their dinner earlier at 7 PM in the evening and they were all sitting around the fire, looking calm and serene outwardly not giving the slightest hint of the huge whirlpool of thoughts that yeas was created in their minds. There was an air of silence-The presence of Kris used to give a kind of heavenly peace to everyone. They did all the hard work with full honestly and determination, now it was time to surrender to God and destiny. There is no short cut or magic to hard work. Nothing in the world can replace it and the brothers knew this precisely. As they say, God helps those who help themselves. Destiny can be changed by attitude, hard work and prayers. This is the belief of a bold and strong person. Weaker ones blame their stars, destiny or whatever it may be called. It is true that one may still not be able to change the outcome even after trying hard very sincerely but that does not rule the option of not trying and giving up on the assumption that one is being ruled by the destiny. The brothers had done everything they could, they cleverly chalked out a training plan, made Aarj learn tricks to control the game not just physically but also mentally by reading opponent's mind. Coach Kris was full of patience and calmness and wanted Aarj to learn mind reading as it's sometimes more important than physical strength. The mind is the ultimate ruler and if one can foresee the next step of the opponent, it may give an opportunity to counter attack it more efficiently.

It's time for the exam now, the preparations were done and the best use of this time could be made only if the brothers could stay cool and away from anxiety or nervousness. A lot of people work very hard but their weak minds may not give the desired results. It's important to control the mind than the mind controlling the human being. The mind can think what we make it think. It's possible!

Night was drawing in and it was time to get some rest. Again, it was not easy to fall asleep quickly like any other day the brothers minds too kept jumping from thought to thought – both desirable and undesirable! It took some time, but soon the brothers fell asleep. However, there was no sleep in the eyes of Aarj and he kept staring at the little night lamp in the corner of the room- contemplating. It was almost 10 PM and the day was supposed to start early. Aarj shrugged off his thoughts as he had to follow a proper sleep routine. He told himself – The time for my victory has come! With a smile on his face, he finally fell asleep.

Night before

It was 5AM, still early in the morning and still a bit dark outside but the brothers woke up and with prayers in their heart, started working on their morning routine.

There was no time to think now, only to act. They got ready. Aarj went for his regular work out, had regular breakfast and the brothers were ready to leave for the stadium. The boxing event was the talk of the town- it was covered very well by the media, newspapers, radio and other agencies.

The D day

The opening ceremony started, and the boxers gathered around. Finally, it was time for the event to begin. Everything went as per schedule. Both Aarj and Duro fought various games against others and they emerged triumphant in all of the games. The scores were very competitive and clearly as expected by the audience, Aarj and Duro were the best boxers. More games as per the schedule took place in the next 4 days. Aarj was easily defeating others and so was the performance of Duro! The whole town was divided into two teams – A Vs D! Quarter finals, semifinals and now it was the time for finals. It was not at all surprising that two best boxers who reached finals were Aarj and Duro.

It was the seventh day of the event and finals were supposed to start in a few hours. Aarj could not forget those hours before the final event. He was experiencing mixed feelings and emotions. Rules were different for the final game- the game could get into dangerous zone as everyone knew how much Duro used to hate Aarj, how he wanted to knock him down and punch until all the ribs were broken. It could lead to permanent disabilities or even death for that matter. They may or may never be able to box again in their lives. It was decided that until one of the boxers ask for help, the game would continue even its leading to serious injuries. Asking for help would mean inviting mockery or accepting defeat. It was not a regular game – Aarj and his brothers' future was on stake and Duro was much full of anger, hatred and jealously that he would rather die but not let Aarj win. Anyways, game had to happen and there is victory waiting for one of them.

Opponents ready

Back at home, Duro's father was sick and could not come to the ring so he asked his close friend Sam to turn on the live video recording and tell what was going on. He could not see properly as his eyes were weak. In his heart, he was praying for his son to win although he knew how unfairly Duro has treated Aarj and his brothers. Not only his outer eyes, but his inner eyes of ethics were also closed. He was blinded in by his love for his son son's and was supportive of every demeaning action of Duro. Sam turned on the video and moved the camera all over. He gave a vivid description of the entire town gathered around in the stadium- friends, family, well-wishers of both teams.

Live telecast

Sam further mentioned Duro was consulting his coach on the boxing strategies, timings, moves and was getting ready for the game. Duro's coach was the Guru of Kris (Aarj's coach) and the irony was now the teacher and the disciple have taken opposite sides. Both the sides were getting ready and their coaches blew the trumpets as part of the rituals. Sound was loud and roaring and the significance was to encourage and give confidence to the boxers. Blowing of these different musical instruments was quite uproarious, vibrating the sky and the earth and it shattered the hearts of Duro and his supporters.

Whistles to blow

It did spark a fear in their hearts as somewhere they knew that they have been unfair to their cousins and the evil may not sustain for a long time against goodness.

Finally, it was the time to go to the ring. Opponents and their team took their places. Duro eyes were burning out of with anger and he was staring at Aarj like a hungry hawk who can't wait to attack his prey. Aarj requested his coach to take him further so he can take a look at the audience, so he could see his relatives and friends and how they were supporting either of the teams. He started looking around, he started seeing how respective team supporters have turned into each other's enemy. He was sad to see this state, he felt he is fighting for something which may lead to everlasting enmity between people and families. While Duro face was full of anger and hatred, Aarj on the other side stood quietly, his face reflecting innocence, a bit of sadness and eyes were looking around as if questioning everyone? It was the moment to stay strong but something happened and Aarj started feeling a bit nervous, a bit perplexed and restless. Kris was quite upset to see this change in Aarj's attitude- this was clearly not the time to turn weak. Very shocking turn of events.

Something wrong with Aarj!!

From here on the rest of the story is divided into 18 parts. These episodes are the conversation between Aarj and Kris as how Aarj got into two minds and is in a confused state and how Kris helps him to come back and perform his duties, regardless of the results.

2

Episode 1- Aarj full of compassion

Aarj – Kris, I see this atmosphere of hatred, anger and enmity which is leading me to depression. I can feel the strength going out of my limbs, my body is quivering and mouth is turning dry. This enmity will run into next coming generations. Are we doing right by getting into this dangerous game of ego and anger?

My whole body is trembling and my hair is standing on end, my gloves are slipping from my hand and I am unable to even stand here. I feel my heart sinking and my skin burning. I am forgetting myself, my mission for last many months and my mind is reeling.

Narration – Aarj put his gloves down and throws himself on the seat. His face down and hands on the head showing how weak he is feeling. He was full of compassion for others. He thinks that for his selfish interest he should not be the cause of enmity and bitterness amongst the people of the town. Even if he wins, he thinks he will not be able to enjoy as after all Duro is his cousin brother, he is family! This game may also lead to the death of one of them or injuries for life time. He thinks he is not scared of dying but he will feel sad if Duro dies in this competition. Aarj thinks wealth to be too trivial and not important enough if it leads to hatred and broken families. Is he right? is it wrong to be compassionate?

Aarj in double mind

Aarj- I do not understand what good will come out of this deadly game of fighting. Now I feel, I do not desire any victory and even if I win, this victory will not give me happiness. I think it's a sin to hurt someone and Duro may get terribly hurt in this game. This is a deadly game and I may not get any pleasure by winning. I will gain some properties, money, riches but at the end of day it's still only money! How can I be so selfish that I am ready to take the life of my own cousin brother for my own interest?

Narration – This is what our mind does to us. Now Aarj is giving all logics as to why he should not play. He being a sportsperson has a moral code to give his best in the game and he is stepping backwards now. He thinks he should just quit boxing and just stay at home and live peacefully with whatever little he gets from his cousin or by earning a humble livelihood. Aarj was demonstrating saintly qualities. But does this kind of saintliness is befitting a sportsperson, especially at that hour? Even if the game is between brothers, one has to play with full efforts and put his heart into it.

Aarj goes to the extent of saying something very unexpected...

Aarj– Further, it was wrong for us to accept this challenge in the first place. We could have further tried to discuss and talk it out. It seems our hearts are overtaken by greed and ego! It's a sin to destroy the family and this is what exactly will happen with one of us winning! Duro is also driven by ego but it's not right for us to also turn into a wrong doer just because the opposite party is. Let them do what they want to, but we should still follow path of peace. After all we are fighting for some share of wealth and even if we win, this wealth which we conquer may or may not stay with us after few years.

Tell me Kris, isn't it wrong to fight with our own people just for the sake of some money or land or riches? We can't stoop down to that level. Its ok, we brother have ability and we can try to earn the wealth separately than getting into this dirty game. Aren't we setting up a wrong example? People will get ideas to fight with each other relatives or kin after seeing this game. This is not right for our society. Tell me, do you think this is called setting of right example?

Narration – Aarj is forgetting his duty as a boxer, as a sportsperson. It's such a shame to have one player refusing to fight because the opponent is his or her sibling! Or two students who are brothers, happen to be in different school and meet each other say in interschool competition. Will they refuse to play or will they refuse to put up their best games just because the opponent is his own brother? Aarj needs to face the ring with sporting spirit. Sad to see this situation now. Where did all the fire and enthusiasm go? He was preparing for this moment for last many months. What about the efforts of the immediate family who helped and supported him whole heartedly and be with him every day, every moment so he can put his best? And this is what now Aarj is thinking! This is a clear example of how powerful our mind and thoughts are and how important it is for us to not become slave of our mind, rather we need to be the master of our mind and use its skill to our best.

All these talks were heard by Sam on the video and he was narrating it to the father of Duro. He further said that, after speaking, Aarj sat in a corner, with his gloves on the side and his mind seemed to be overwhelmed with grief. Duro's father did not show any expression but Sam knew that he was happy in his heart. If Aarj does not fight, Duro will win. His father was blinded in son's love, not trying to get his son on the right path. He was also responsible as he could not give right upbringing and turned Duro into an evil person.

3

Episode 2- What is more important? One's duty or being compassionate?

Narration – After hearing Aarj and seeing his depressed state of mind, eyes full of tears, pale skinned, this is what Kris said.

Kris – How come this came to you at the wrong time? You were never like this. I am surprised to see this weak state of yours. Look at all of your well-wishers and brothers. They have high hopes from you and at this point you are becoming faint hearted! Get up and fight. This is what your duty is right now.

Aarj – I cannot think of fighting my uncle's son. I take him as my brother. Even if I fight and I emerge victorious, I won't enjoy that victory as my consciousness will not let me take pleasure in the defeat of my brother. What pleasure will I get by making other's sad? Better to live as poor and on alms than to live a life of riches like this.

Narration – How manipulating our mind can get and it may come up with all sort of reasoning. One of the most capable boxers is now thinking of backing out from tournament because of these illogical reasons which he thinks to be quite valid. The situation is quite remorse and very disappointing. People will call Aarj coward if he backs out but he thinks he is being compassionate to his opponent and he does not want to hurt him. What an unbelievable analogy!

Kris- Aarj, you try to talk like a sensible and intelligent person but actually what you are saying is completely non-sense. As a boxer, what is your duty? Why are you worried about what will happen after the game is over? You just have to play your best and leave the rest on destiny. Do you think yourself as the controller of all events in your life? You cannot, you just cannot. All you need to do is to what is right. Maybe you come up as a winner but then would be the time to get compassionate and be nice towards the other side. But definitely not right now! It's good to carry compassion in your heart, but what's the point of carrying compassion for the dress of the drowning man?

Narration – Aarj did want to understand what Kris was trying to explain but his mind was grappled up in his own thoughts and he was not able to think straight. He asked Kris to be his mentor and guide him. He kept giving arguments that even if he wins, he won't be able to live happily so there is no point in fighting. Saying this and with tears in his eyes, he just declared to Kris – *"I wont fight this game, I just can't!"*.

Kris (smilingly)- Don't be foolish, my friend! You give logics like a learned person, but you don't act like wise ones. Give up this petty weakness of your heart. You have grabbed numerous boxing championship awards in the past, how is this different?

Winning and losing are two sides of a coin. One of the outcome is inevitable. You should not worry about the results now. It's time to act, not to grieve. If you refuse to fight now, you will be a piece of mockery amongst all and it's better to fight and lose than to live a life of a coward. One who gives up is not respected by the society! This is worse than losing as in that case you just lose the game but not your reputation.

You should treat victory and defeat, gain and loss, joy and sorrow alike and get ready for the final game. Do not get nervous now. Even if you lose, you will have the satisfaction that you tried your best! You will think high of yourself later in life.

Go, get up and fight and keep calm all the time. In times of extreme sorrow or even extreme happiness, stay calm and this is what is called getting victory over the emotions which overwhelm us. It's different to enjoy emotions but it's dangerous to get indulged in those emotions. This is also a kind of yoga and one of the best yoga that you can practice.

Let me give you an example – a soldier who is fighting against the enemy country cannot put his gun down and say- "Oh, violence and blood shed is bad for mankind. I don't think we should kill each other". This is quite illogical.

Narration – Kris was absolutely surprised and shocked to see this state of Aarj. This was something which they were practicing and preparing for vigorously and suddenly this turn of events that Aarj simply refused to fight!! It was very disappointing for Kris. Other brothers had no idea what was going on in Aarj mind and they were watching excitedly all game preparations. Kris was trying his best to change Aarj mind.

Whats wrong Aarj?

Kris- You are worried if Duro would get hurt badly or if he would die? What does that have to do with the game? Where is that fighting spirit? Adhere to the rules of the game, be fair with each other and let's embrace the outcome. I am not saying its right to kill people or injure them but its ethical to fight for your own rights and in that process if you abide by all rules and still someone gets hurt, let it be. When one has to die, he or she will. Who has taken birth here, can't avoid the death. This is a very strong statement and this should not be used in a manipulative way. You need to focus on discharging your duties. As I mentioned earlier, if an enemy nation is attacking us, would our military sit quietly giving these arguments that oh! blood shed is not good! Why can't we avoid it? Let's give them the land they want to encroach on or money or our people and let's live peacefully! Most foolish thing to do or say or also seems to very cowardice.

When there is a war between nations for the just cause, people do die. So, if they die, they may take birth again as per the theory of reincarnation which you may or may not believe in. Let the cycle go on, you just need to stand as a fair and truthful man.

Kris further added – Lucky are those sportsmen who get these kinds of opportunities. My dear famous boxer, either you will conquer or you will get conquered but in neither circumstance, you should give up. Get up and fight, for the sake of fighting and not for the sake of consequences. They will follow. Victory or defeat- one of them is yours.

Less intelligent people keep giving the reasoning which you are giving right now. Be free of this anxiety, stay calm and do what is your duty in this hour.

Listen to this carefully- This was told **_5,000 years back_** and still true-

"You have an obligation to perform your duty, not a right to have your desired fruits of action". This way you will not feel extreme sorrow in life.

Aarj- This is quite difficult to follow. Do those kinds of people exist who can give up their desires and can find satisfaction in any situation? If yes, tell me who are they? How are they so evolved? They must be cut from a different cloth as they can't fit in our fabric of societal norms.

Kris- Its simple- those people do exist, although they are rare. Anyone who can understand this logic will be able to follow it. Only thing I can tell you is that their mind is mostly calm- they don't fall into attachment of various things, they don't fear anything and they are free from anxieties of life. You don't see them weeping loudly when something goes wrong or laughing hysterically when things go their way. It's all related, when there is too much possessiveness for something, an attachment arises and then it leads to frustration which in turn may lead to anger. Anger leads to delusion and we lose the ability to think clearly and thus again fall into the trap of taking wrong decisions and then repentance.

Have you ever observed sportsmen? How some of them have controlled actions and reactions under any circumstances whereas others sway like a pendulum and are happy when things are fine but get supremely agitated and angry throwing tantrums when things don't go their way

They lose their ability to think logically and very likely will take wrong decisions. Why is MS Dhoni respected so much for maintaining his cool always, even during the most strenuous and pressurizing times? He may have taken right or wrong decisions, that is different but the calmness of mind gave him an opportunity to think logically and straight.

Senses are very strong. e.g. A person having diabetes should keep himself away from sweets but the moment he sees a chocolate lava cake, he may fall for its temptation. Like how the boat on the water is swept by a strong wind, similarly our mind can carry away our intelligence.

So, in conclusion, those people who have given up their attachment or desires can alone attain real peace. This does not mean that we should not work for what one desires, it just says that work hard and accept the outcome whole heartedly. This is also a ticket to travel to higher and better planets – how? I will explain another time.

4

Episode 3- Simple mantra

Aarj- Thanks Kris, I think I can understand what you are trying to tell me but the knowledge or wisdom that you are giving me says that I should be happy with every situation in life and at the same time you are asking me to fight. I am more confused. Why should I fight if I just try to understand this wisdom that let destiny take control of things and lets not worry about the results? Tell me what is easy to understand.

Narration – What would be easy to understand for even an ordinary person is proving most confusing for Aarj because his ability to think and reason is clouded. Perhaps he is looking for an excuse to cancel the fight. Let's see how Kris tries to explain him again. This is what a good friend does. Trying to pull the friend towards right things in life and showing the correct path. We all get lost at times and this is when we need a true friend or a mentor or a guide who can show us the right way.

Kris- Aarj, knowledge and action both are required. You cannot stay without doing any work, so action is there but carry it on with wisdom that you are not bound with results. Perform your duties in the light of the knowledge. So, there are two paths – path of action and path of knowledge.

Even if you understand one path and move on it, you will have peace in life. If you are not interested in gaining deep knowledge, then just perform your duty as called for it. E.g. if you are a student, you need to make sure your home work is submitted in time, you are ready for assessments and when you are a sportsperson, let's make sure you reach dot on time for your physical training, practice etc. It's as simple as that. Be sincere in what you do and do not try to avoid and find an escape.

The whole point is to tell you to put in your 100% and then do not worry about the results. If you are just thinking of the results that how you should win the trophy or how you should graduate with glowing marks, then that's not enough. Action has to take place. You need to practice for hours and hours to flair in your sport, or music or anything that you want to excel in.

Simple mantra for people believing in action is – perform action in 100% right way but do not worry about the outcome. Do your best and leave rest on the nature.

Control your desires if they delude you or if they take you away from the goal. For example, if your goal is to reduce weight then it's important for you to resist the ice cream even if your friend is eating right in front of you. This is called controlling your desires or senses for the wrong things.

Because man has started having uncontrollable desires, it's also leading to environment degradation. Slowly by developing these qualities, we will also be doing good to mother nature. If every person just takes the right share for him/her and not get influenced by greed then there will be a harmony amongst all living as well as non-living beings in the nature.

Aarj - Yes, I would want to be best in what I am doing – be it running the business or be the best boxer in the world. I don't want to waste my life in doing menial jobs, especially sometimes my mom asks me to mop the house, wash dishes etc.

Kris – This is where you go wrong Aarj. No job is big or small or significant or insignificant. Let me tell you a remarkable incident from America's late president, Abraham Lincoln's life. Once other senators in the parliament, made fun of Lincoln's father as he was a cobbler. The work of cobbler was supposed to be considered as a low-grade job. Lincoln with no shame, rather with a hint of pride, replied back saying – "I hope as a President, I can be as good in my work as my father was as a cobbler". He asked the other Senators to point out one mistake in their shoes which were made by his father.

A peon or a carpenter or a plumber Is much better than a director or officer of the company if he is performing his job with perfection and sincerity. This is what makes a man satisfied and slowly the fame comes their way. Even if it does not, it should not matter as the work performed with honesty and sincerity is not to attain fame, but this is a way of discharging our duty towards nature. We all need to work in harmony to maintain balance at home, at school, at office and in society.

Feeling compassionate- at this hour?

Everyone has a duty to serve the society in their own ways – look at the service rivers are providing or mountains or even desserts for that matter. Imagine a super power which is running the universe and all these suppliers of essential necessities of life such as air, water, metals, sunlight, moonlight, rainfall is governed by the agents of that super power or in simple words subordinates of the super power. Around the world, in lots of countries or religions these agents are worshipped or tried to be pleased, e.g. farmers in India trying to please rain God so it rains adequately and timely in order for them to have a good harvest.

Narration - Point which Kris is trying to make here we do enjoy all these free facilities given by nature to us, so let's make sure to give something back to the nature by respecting it, by not abusing or stealing from nature. A society of thieves will always be punished by mother nature and we have already witnessed the climate change and other natural calamities due to human intervention.

These days environmentalists talk about the same thing which was already spoke some **5,000 years back**. Mother nature was not exploited as that was not the era of machines, but still the awareness was there.

Even the food we eat, comes from rain, soil and sunlight etc. These are all nature's agents. Let's give them respect by eating only pure food which is meant to be eaten. Anything we try to do against the law of nature will come back as boomerang in the form of epidemic or chronic diseases or other fatalities. This is why in ancient civilizations, there was a practice to worship lord of rain or air or water and by having that reverence one does not think of exploiting these resources. We get humbler in using those for our benefit. Mother nature and living beings live in harmony with each other.

Let's talk about the services one can offer. If you are a businessman and you are running business in all ethical ways, you are doing good to the society. This is also a service.

It's better to perform our role in the society even if not in perfection than to perform someone's else role with perfection.

Duty of a plumber is as important as a duty of a CEO of a company. If everyone becomes CEO, then may be becoming a plumber would be considered as high-level profession. So, whatever is our duty, should be followed.

Even great kings or leaders who had lots of riches and power, had to work and discharge their duties. They did work hard all their life in spite of being at the top position. Work never stops, whatever your duty is you should do. In fact, general public will follow their leaders or rulers. If you are a leader and you are preaching against smoking and you yourself smoke, do you think you are setting a right example? Those kinds of people are the greatest cheaters and they just sway the innocent public.

Aarj is a world-renowned boxer, if he just refuses to play he is sending a wrong message to the entire world who looks upon him or take him as their ideal. This is why Kris spoke about leadership qualities.

Aarj – This all if fine Kris, but I see a lot of people, seemingly quite intelligent and wise but still committing sin! Why is it like that?

Kris - Because of anger in them. Anger and greed leads to lot of devastation. One should stay calm in every situation and then handle it.

Imagine if there is a fire in the room and its covered with smoke, will you be able to see the furniture and other things clearly? This is how our mind works when we are hooked upon on some desire, e.g. whatever happens I need Xbox newest version! And when the same child grows up into a young man, then may be that Xbox desire turns into a desire for a sports car!

And non-fulfillment of the desire will lead to anger, which in turn leads to delusion and in that cloud of delusion, we don't see things clearly.

5

Episode 4- What happened 120 million years ago?

———❤———

Aarj – But Kris, how do you know about all this stuff? They never taught us this in school. From where did you get this understanding?

Kris- This understanding is thousands and thousands of years old. Creator of the universe gave this knowledge to Sun God and then it was passed on to next generations but it lost in between. And then approx. **<u>5,000 years ago</u>**, again this knowledge was talked about in some dynasty. I know all about it through various means and thus I am telling you.

Aarj- What are you talking about? That sounds like a fantasy world. Are you sure what you are saying is right as it's just not making any sense to me. Creator? Who is the creator? And it all sounds weird that there is a sun god and all.

How do you know that knowledge was given to Sun God millions of years back? You were not there to vouch all that and still you seem to say as if you have seen all this happening. Are you talking about some sci-fi thing where people can go back in time or jump into future on time machines? It all sounds like some fictional story.

Kris- Let me tell you the history of the creation of this universe. Creator or the super power first created Sun. Sun was created hundreds of millions of years back. Creator has its own agents who were busy getting earth ready for human civilization. Sun had already come into existence. They called that era to be Manu era. Manu Era started 305 million years back and some 120 million years back Sun demigod spoke about this knowledge.

Human civilization started very 4.3 million years back which seem to be long time ago but relatively it may be considered as recent when compared with a total history of 305 million years. People are surprised as we know about only last few thousand years of events but I have read and found from various sources that its actually quite old than we think. Let's divide the time since civilization evolved on earth into existence into 4 different parts.

That itself in total cannot be considered as the total life of the earth as right now we are talking only about the time period of civilization. Earth is millions of years older than this.

Total human civilization era on earth = Part1 + Part2 + Part3 + Part4

Now let's look into the no. of years which makes these different parts.

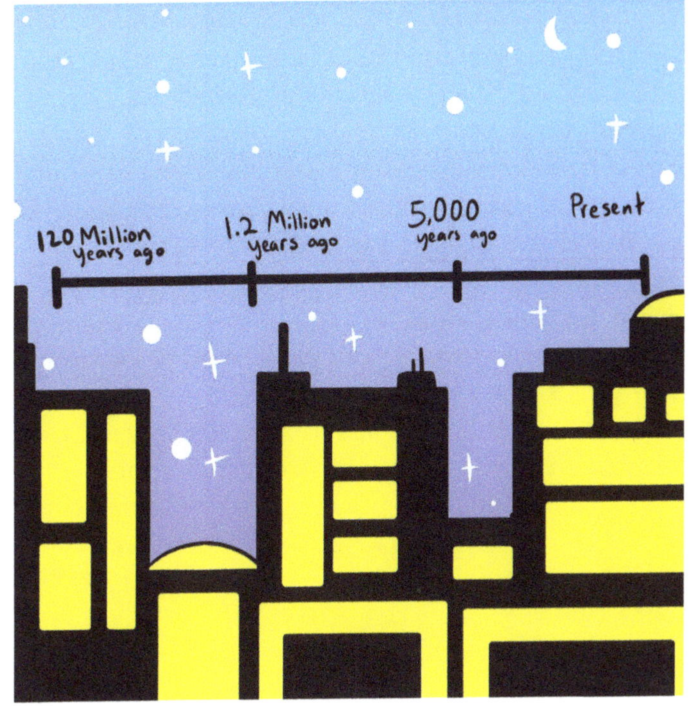

Timeless timeline

History of human civilization –

Part 1 (Golden Era) = 1,728,000 years

Part 2 = 1,296,000 years (knowledge was given to the King of earth)

Part 3 = 864,000 years

Part 4 (Darkness Era, still running) = 432,000 years (spoken by a friend to another friend)

Going with these numbers, first time this knowledge was talked about was approx. 120 million years ago, 2nd time same info was given to King of Earth some 1.2Mn. years back and third time it was heard 5,000 years back. I am just repeating the same words now.

This knowledge is actually a very high-level science and it can be understood by only those who have certain kind of intelligence to look beyond what their eyes can see.

Even though we must have lived in say Part 1 of the time period I mentioned but we don't remember all this as a normal human being can only live for 90-100 years and then we die and we forget all that had happened in our earlier life. We come back as a baby and again start living. This way we have also lived millions of years but we can't remember all that has happened in our past lives. What to say about past lives, sometimes we don't even remember what happened few days back or even few hours back. This is how bad our memory is.

Human beings have propensity to cheat each other and when these evil crosses all limits, sometimes nature has to intervene to make sure righteousness prevails over injustice. This is what is happening now. By defeating evil Duro, you will establish the victory of good over evil and we all will help you achieve it.

Aarj- I feel I am dreaming. It does not sound like real. Tell me why do we need to take birth again and again? What was I in my previous birth? Was I a better boxer then? Can you tell me?

Kris- You have had thousands and millions of births. You were a fish, then a plant, animal and after 8.4 million births, now you have become a human being. What you are saying is right. By taking birth again and again, we go through the life cycle of pleasure and pain, happiness and sorrow every time. A common man would not even question it and they would think this is what it is, just live life. But if one understands this concept, one can start questioning more on this mechanism, get deeper into it and try to get a meaning out of this system.

Various stages

There are lots of planets in our universe. Earth is not a very sophisticated planet to be on. We can see there is lot of suffering and miseries around us. Can you imagine a planet where all inhabitants always live happy, healthy, young and a rich life? That should be the case ALWAYS! Very hard to imagine as we have never seen something like that.

This life of ours on Earth is like a video game. We play good, we pass a stage and we get promoted to the higher stage. Similarly, we live good and we try to move to a better planet.

Aarj – I still don't understand what are you talking about? This all feels like a fiction. You are my friend but the way you are talking, seems like you are part of some intelligence group of the super power who is ruling all this. From where are you getting all these ideas? Are they part of some imaginative story?

Kris- You just need to understand with a full dedicated mind. Get rid of confusion, anger, fear and any other ill thought. Then you can acquire more understanding. Once again, I am reiterating that you need to follow your duty. I may go bit more general in my explanation now, but let me tell you why following one's duty is important.

Our entire society can be divided into four working classes. First class is of highly educated and intelligent people, second class is of bureaucrats which will include army as well, third class is of business and enterprising people and fourth are service providers. Each one of them has to do their work diligently and then society can balance itself well. No work is less important than other. It may seem like some people are more respected than others but every person's work is equally important and there could be a chaos if some of them are not working in harmony with others. E.g. labor may not be considered as highly reputed or elite but if they go on strike, the entire society is affected.

So, right now your work is to perform as a boxer. So, I would suggest strongly that you go and fight against your opponent without worrying about the results. Just do your best. Your action should not be dependent on the outcome. Rather your action should reveal that you are putting in your 200%. Accept the results whether its victory or defeat and continue working on improving your performance. That's the true sportsmanship. Be in the state of equanimity.

Now coming back to the question, you raised – Why do we need to take birth again and again? You must be thinking if there is a so called higher planet, wont it be nice if we can just travel to that planet where everything is so advanced, no virus attacks, no health problems and one does even get old there?

And my answer is, yes of course you can. You can live a better life there where we don't spend time in petty fights and unnecessary arguments. But there is a way to reach to that planet and nothing comes without hard work. The law of this system says that if one is discharging his/her duty in an honest way, you will soon be teleported from Earth to this super shining planet. This is self-illuminating planet and it is not dependent on any sun. This is how powerful it is.

Once again, don't procrastinate and think of every task as your duty and don't get worried or fearful of anything. If you always live in this knowledge, perform your duties without your selfish interest, you won't be tied to lower planet like earth.

You are a part of that super energy which is running the world and you don't need to get weak or nervous at this time. Come on, get up and go in the ring.

6

Episode 5 – Aarj confusion stays, what is better–knowledge or action?

———❧———

Narration – Aarj is confused again. He is asking if he should focus on gaining more knowledge or just perform his work devotedly. Both methods are desirable. If he gains more knowledge, he will understand the intricacies of nature better. Or he should not worry about getting deeper into this knowledge and rather focus on his duties. Which path is more preferable and easy to work upon?

Aarj- Hi Kris, I am sorry but you made me confused again. You just said learn about this knowledge and its quite important as it will help us understand the whole science behind earth and other planets. But then again you said that knowledge is fine, but just focus on doing your work with full sincerity and not worry about anything else. As a human being, we can't do it all. What should I focus on?

Shall I just leave all this and go to a school to learn more about the nature and super power or shall I just continue what I am doing?

Kris- Both paths are good. Once you gain knowledge, you will understand how nature works. You can get following questions answered. What are you here for? How should you act in different circumstances? It may be a little difficult path as you will need to put in lot of time studying it.

The easier path is just understanding the role you are playing in life and perform it with full devotion. Right now, you are a boxer, so just go and fight. When you are playing role of a student, do what is expected of you. When you are with a friend, behave like one and not like a son which you would when you are with your parents. This path is less difficult to practice, so may be easier to follow. Contemplation is not for everyone but everyone does perform actions so let's make sure actions befit the circumstances and the role.

It's very important for a sportsperson or a student to manage their stress and anxiety. One can be at peace only when one accepts the outcomes. But that does not mean that one should not perform the hard work. Nothing can substitute the hard work. Even after putting in your best, one may come up to negative results. Let's accept that as law of nature and move on. That way one can always be happy within, always in the state of bliss and equanimity. Depression cannot even touch that person. Keep working day and night but let's be free from anger, desires, greed or fear. That kind of person is considered to be a true yogi.

7

Episode 6- Trick to stay cool!

❦

Narration- Aarj wants to know the trick of how to stay cool and calm and just keep doing his duty without getting perturbed.

Aarj- Hi Kris, it's very nice to hear what all you are saying but still very hard to implement. Even after listening to you, I feel I am not still ready for boxing game as I feel sad from inside. I feel there is no point hitting mercilessly my own cousin and that too just for the sake of some wealth. It's just not convincing enough for me.

On other note, you mention that one should stay and work like yogi but tell me how can one control his mind and heart. It's very difficult for a common person. We all do what our mind asks us to do and its almost next to impossible to go against our mind's wishes.

One prepares so hard for an event all his life and you are asking sportsperson and students to not worry about the outcome and just focus on your hard work. Hard work is done ONLY to get desired outcome so how is it possible to not focus on outcome? What is the point of doing hard work itself then?

Kris- Very apt questions Aarj! It's so right for you to ask these as I do agree with you that it's not an easy path. Have you seen ascetics performing austerities for years and years? They clad themselves in a piece of cloth and spend cold winters as well as summers that way. They take limited food and water and try to control their mind by performing those yoga. Well, anything that one does sincerely, gives results. I am not saying anything against them but I do want to make a point that better than those ascetics, is the one common man who is living in the midst of this day to day world and still thinking and living like a yogi in his mind. A person who is able to control the unnecessary desires of senses is better than the person who is spending half of his life in some cave in Himalayas and trying to contemplate and meditate.

You asked me what is the way to control the mind? I would say try meditation. Do it the right way and conquer your mind. This is a very effective technique. This is how a person can become controlled, calm and raise above praises and insults, success and failure etc. Gradually one's attitude stays equal and he has equal vision towards well-wishers, family, friends or even enemies. Mind if controlled, can become one's best friends, else it can be an enemy also.

Another scientific fact is that one can't stay calm if one eats too much or too little or sleeps too much or too little. A balanced approach is required.

No doubt it is difficult but by constant practice and efforts, it is achievable. Set up a goal and focus and work towards it. "***Never give up***" is the key! And this formula for success is timeless and universal.

Stay cool- whatever be the situation

And these qualities that you develop in this life time can also be carried forward to next birth and you may get next birth say in a very wealthy family or in a yogi family, depending upon your karmas in this life time.

***Aarj*-** Yogi family? Would that mean who wakes up early morning, does some bodily and breathing exercises, can demonstrate lots of flexibility and agility and can perform various gymnastics as well? Sure, that person is healthy most of the time.

Kris said laughingly- "No, that's not called yoga, this is just a part of yoga. People have started understanding yoga and yogi in a different way. This is not even close to the real meaning. Let me tell you who is a yogi- A yogi is a person who has learnt to control his mind, who has learnt to control his desires and one who can stay calm in all situations. To such a person, happiness and sorrow, heat and cold, honor and dishonor are all the same. It's an extremely difficult stage and it cannot be attained by reading books or writing exams on Yoga. It can come only by constant practice but it's possible. Even if we attain this kind of mental equilibrium for a small part of our life, we should consider ourselves to be lucky.

Aarj- (after thinking for few seconds) This again sounds good and desirable in theory but it's really difficult to implement. This seems to be impractical Kris. May be its easier to control wind than really control the mind as thoughts come gushing in mind, sometimes it stays calm, sometimes it gets restless. Seems quite difficult and almost impossible.

Kris- You are right, it's difficult ...may be almost impossible but not impossible. Think of it this way. Let me give you an analogy. Let's think this body of ours is like a car, we (inner self or soul) are the passenger, our intelligence is the driver (driver needs to think how to reach to destination), car's steering, accelerator, brakes, clutch etc. are all part of mind. Our intelligence need to be able to master these driving instruments so we can use it properly and make sure we are reaching our destination. But if the steering says, oh I feel like making a left turn as the road really looks nice and beautiful there and really don't care about anything else and if we give up to its demands, then we don't know where we land. We need to follow the map and go in the right direction. We may just get lost if we don't follow the map.

In this case, we can ignore what mind is asking and continue to go on our path. It might be not easy to resist making a left turn but with constant practice and determination we can do that. We need to be a bit detached and not make a left turn where it looks rosy and green but continue on the path which may not be looking like fun but we know as per our map, that's the right way to go.

8

Episode 7- One in million will be special

---◇---

Aarj- Tell me more about this age-old timeless tip that you are talking about. Tell me all in detail as I am still very confused. You seem to put things in very simple way but it's actually quite difficult.

Kris- Ok, fine. Let me try to get into more details. If you really understand this which is still a mystery for majority of the human kind, you would know the essence of all my talks. Nothing more would be more important than this.

First, let me tell you that hardly one in million would show interest in these talks. Out of those millions, will inquire and out of those further few would be rare souls who would want to implement this in their lives. The fact that you are even asking makes you ahead in intelligence than most of the people.

Now let's talk about how human body is consisting of various energies. It consists of material energies and spiritual energies. Material energy is comprised of five elements which are earth, water, fire, air and sky. It also consists of three other internal elements which is mind, intelligence and our ego. These eight elements combine together and form material energy. Our body material is made up of these eight elements.

Spiritual energy is the one which gives life to the person. All human beings who are alive have both spiritual and material energies and this is how they operate. Spiritual energy is considered to be superior and material energy is inferior. So, in essence human beings are superior in nature (as we have both material and spiritual energy) and the matter is inferior. Matter can be gross such as earth or water or it can be subtle e.g. mind or intelligence. We tend to exploit material energies and try to find happiness but that pleasure is inferior as it comes out of material energies.

Now let's think, where is the spiritual energy coming from? It's coming from a place which is an energy store house. Someone energetic can only give us energy. If we truly understand this superior energy, then we realize that day to day stuff that we worry about are of not much importance in life. So right now, you are worrying about material energy factors and this is why I am telling you that there is nothing to be concerned of.

Aarj- who is this "energetic" that you are referring to? What energy store house are you talking about?

Kris- That is something which is omnipresent. Like light in sun or taste of water or smell of earth or brilliance of fire. All kind of qualities such as goodness or passion or even evil nature or just ignorance/carelessness arise out of this energy. But the energy is above everything –it can be used to give us good or bad things in life. Energy in itself will not be good or bad. It depends how we use it. Like for example, a gangster may use a gun to kill innocent people and police may use the same gun to protect people.

Aarj- What kind of people would be interested in even knowing things that you are talking about? It all sounds so complicated and am not sure if anyone would even want to think about that superior energy.

Kris- Every person has an inherent and in-born nature. Some people are born with more of selfish or evil nature and it's no point making them understand or even telling them about all this. It will be a waste of time.

I will tell you about four kinds of people who will probably not take interest in this high-class intelligence which we are talking about.

First kind of people are usually workaholics - they work day and night without realizing where they are heading towards. It's not wrong to work day and night as lot of people probably can't control their work hours and they would be required to in order to support themselves, their families and so on. But the awareness may be lacking. They may spend sleepless days and nights, accumulating wealth or recognition and also making their body a home of various diseases. Their intelligence stops at the level of earning material gains and respect for themselves by reaching to an elite position. That's the goal of their life.

Second kind of people are those who are socially and politically developed but missing spiritual component. They don't work just for themselves. Maybe they are helping society or doing a great service to mankind but they have forgotten their true spiritual nature.

Third kind of people are those who are very well read, philosophers, scholars but those are pseudo intellectuals. They can very well argue on the topics they have read on but they don't want to acknowledge the real knowledge based on which the entire creation is dependent.

Fourth kind of people are those who openly call themselves non-believer in spiritual energy and they feel proud about it. They will never take interest in these kinds of talks.

Now moving on to the next four kinds who are in my opinion, would probably be interested in these talks.

First, one who is very distressed, as it's nature of the human to go and ask for help from that superior energy or God! Let imagine a situation when the doctors give up, people would usually go to temples or churches to ask for blessings. This is when they think that there is someone superior to them who can probably do wonders.

Secondly, seekers of wealth would want to pray and ask for more riches. They will recognize there is a super power and would want to request them to endow them with wealth. They may need wealth or power or respect or recognition and accordingly they wish for, they perform prayers to please that particular God and they may also get their wish become true. They may put tremendous faith in their belief. This happens across religions, across countries and across cultures.

Third, someone who is curious to know more. For e.g. if I am telling you all this, you are curious to know more and this is why you are questioning me.

Fourth are the rare people who have this wisdom. Those are very few people in the world who have understood this truth and they are wise enough to take shelter under this energy.

Try to become like that wise person. Other three may not continue to understand more once their desires are fulfilled or once their curiosity is satisfied at any level. This kind of intelligence or wisdom does not come so easily. It's our spiritual treasure that we are accumulating and carrying from one life to the other.

Speaking of treasure or wealth, there are two kinds of treasures – material and spiritual.

Material treasure is what a person accumulates lifelong and it could be bank balance, properties, jewellery, cars etc. Once the person dies, everything stays here and he cannot take anything with him. We are talking about materialistic knowledge, that say a doctor or engineer has earned by working hard on those degrees. This knowledge also does not get passed on to next life. When body dies, it gets buried with it.

Spiritual treasure is the knowledge that we gain by understanding it, it's called the real wisdom.

Spiritual knowledge sits on the spirit and once the rebirth happens, same spirit finds a new body. It still has that knowledge and once brushed up, the person can start from the level he stopped in his previous birth. That's not the case with material knowledge. We again have to start from kindergarten, again start accumulating wealth and in the end, leave it all here.

Try to become like the fourth kind of person who carries true wisdom. He/she knows what their duty is and they don't get confused about it. If you have this wisdom, you would know that now you should go in the ring and follow the religion of a sports person.

Remember I even told you about various levels of planets – More higher level or sophisticated planet where one does not fall sick, does not feel sad and they don't even get old. They enjoy the vigor of youth all the time. Our aim should be to reach to that highest planet. Why would you want to go and stay in a local mediocre hotel if you can afford to book a room in a five star one! Those who can understand this analogy, they may be able to understand further.

9

Episode 8- Mystery of re-birth and cosmic travel

Narration – It seems like Aarj was gradually understanding Kris point of view but still in no possible ways his curiosity was coming down. In fact, he was asking more and more questions. This tells us that there is nothing wrong in asking questions – even if we feel that they are the stupidest of all! May be its better to ask than to assume something utterly wrong.

Aarj- you mentioned that spiritual knowledge gets transferred to the new body as well, when re birth happens. Rebirth happens only when the person leaves the current body. As per what you said, that's when the spirit finds a new body and starts living in there. So, you mean to say spirit or soul never gets old? Won't it also need some rest like how we do? When our bodies get old and we can't do the same actions with as much vigor as we used to do when we were young.

Also, I see people dying around all the time. Some die of natural cause, some of accidents, some of diseases or pandemics etc. Does that also matter in deciding how the soul finds a new body?

Kris (laughingly)- Aarj, you keep asking questions and some of them are worthy spending time on.

Yes, soul never ever gets old – it will have same form and quality of what it had millions of years ago. It's only our body which goes through birth, diseases, old age and finally death. These four phenomena are applicable only to this material body which will not last forever and this is why you should understand about soul as it was there millions of years back and it will always exist.

We need to understand how it jumps from one body to another and why is that your soul got body of Aarj and not Yuvi or not Duro? There is a science behind all this. It does not happen by co incidence. There is a proper process and this is how it takes place.

Let me tell you some more interesting facts-

Let me tell you how important our thoughts are, more important and impactful than actions at times. They say – what we think, we become. This is quite true in what I am going to explain next. The kind of body that we may get in next birth depends upon our karma in the present birth and our thoughts at the time when our soul was departing from the existing body.

Some wise people may ask – why do we even get into this loop of birth, death, rebirth and again birth, death and rebirth. Why can't we just stop all this? Every time we take birth, we need to go to school again, we need to appear for entrance exams again, we need to win some competitions, make it into a good college, start earning, have families, kids, start savings for their education and self-retirement, hope to have a healthy life at the last stage and finally depart. Isn't this we doing over and over, again and again for ages? Is there any way to stop it?

Yes, there is a way to stop it. But for that, the above knowledge is needed and faith in the process explained here. Now, I will tell you another secret here which very few people know on this planet.

"Thinking of whatever entity, one leaves the body at the time of the death, that and that alone one attains being ever absorbed in its thought".

Let me tell you one story that I have heard about King Bharat. This was like many hundreds of years back. In his old age, king left the kingdom and went to forests to spend his remaining time meditating upon the super power. Every day he would go to the lake to take bath. There he saw a fawn whose mother has died while giving birth. He took the fawn with him and took care of him and slowly got attached to him. When he was dying, the thought of the fawn (now it was a grown-up deer) came to his mind and thus after his death, he again took birth on this planet only. But his birth was in animal kingdom and he was a deer. He remembered his last birth and also realized the mistake he made.

We may convince ourselves- oh when that final moment comes, I will think of something good or I may think of this "super energetic" person referred in the previous chapter or I may think of this "Secret knowledge". Do you really think we may remember? Death may come in a fraction of second and everything could change in that one second. From where would our mind remember to think of this and to avoid thinking of something else? Suddenly, we may think of our dog- oh what will happen to my dear doggy once I am gone and boom. you may get the body of a dog in next birth!! Of course, you may get comfortable life like some rich family adopting you if you had done good karmas rather than life of a street dog which spends hours and hours looking for the crumbs of food near trash cans!

So, lets train ourselves, lets train our minds to think of something worthy at that final moment. Think of that as final assessment and lets constantly prepare ourselves for that. Let's be conscious of that truth at the back of our mind all the time, even when we are busy partying, busy playing, busy watching movie or feeling sad or depressed. We can't have same emotions all the time – Feelings of sorrow, happiness, excitement, contentment, desires etc. may come and may go. Regardless, let's make sure that our foundation is built up on this and only "meaningful knowledge" so we can just not plan for our retirement in this birth but also for our future births.

Now let's look at various ways of training our mind. There are different ways and you can just adopt one which you believe in most. They are all good and all will take us to the same conclusion.

Solution 1- Simplest

Easiest and simplest for any layman, even for the most average person is constantly remembering the name of the God or super energetic person. Imagine if a person does that for sixty years of his life, every day for few minutes or for few hours, won't it become a habit? Won't it become a part of his routine? Chances are that he will do the same in that final moment and he would be able to crack the exam. This is the simplest way. Isn't it?

Solution 2- Need some efforts

Second way to control our mind is to meditate. There are various places one can learn to meditate and with constant practice, one can try to control unwanted thoughts and focus on the right ones. We can even meditate on the spark which we have within ourselves, absence of which person will be called dead. Do you know how small that is? May be 1/10,000th part of the tip of the hair!

These two are the simplest, easiest and common methods.

Bit difficult ones are to get further deep into knowledge and read hundreds of books written on it but one may not feel interested in studies.

Aarj- my head is spinning with all this information you are giving. I don't know how to comprehend them. One questions that comes to my mind- "Isn't there some mid-way around? Like you mentioned either we come back on the earth in the form of animals, plants or human beings or we just get away from that cycle". You make it sound easy but it's really not easy to train the mind and have those controlled thoughts at the final moment in order to be able to get away from rebirth. So, we have only two options?

Kris- Again I must say you got a good question. Let me tell you this creation is much and much bigger than what our minds can interpret. You think there is only one planet earth, where there is life, right? No, there are thousands of other planets too which are habitat of other living creatures. This is actually a science and not sci-fi. We only went to moon and mars and figured there is no one there but those two celestial bodies are not even a fraction of .01% of total universe or I should say multiverse. Living beings from earth can get transported to other planets also at the time of rebirth. Those planets have different days and nights or the different duration of day and night.

Let me give you two examples –

There is cosmic planet quite far from here and at much heights and it is said that their 12 hours is equal to 4.32

billion years of earth. So, imagine their one day which is also 24 hours would be equivalent to 8.64 billion years!!! And that planet has extra super medicinal powers that doesn't let its habitants fall sick. It's a prosperous place and thus full of enjoyment. They may live up to 70-80 years of life but in our earth years it may come to billions and trillions! It looks like a pretty long and comfortable life but from the view point of eternity, it is as short as a **lightning flash**. It will still come to an end sometime, some day and then what? Take birth again and that time may be back on earth or some other planet.

Similarly, there is another planet whose one day is equivalent to 15 days of our time! Their one year could be approx. 28-29 earth years!

In short, answer is – there are various planets and in hierarchy! Like if you work hard and live a good life and are successful you may afford a place in one of the richest high rise of New York or you may have to settle with something less. The way we move and make progress in this life, similarly our soul also progresses. But there is another difference. In this life, people may cheat and may not let us have what we deserve even if we are honest or hard working but that does NOT happen with the journey of soul. No one can control it except the nature and there is no disturbance from anyone else. So, the soul will move to higher planets depending upon how realized it is.

We talked about those two planets. Let me tell you about the supreme one. This is the place which is where super power is rising. And there is no coming back from that place. That's the fun part of being there. It does not end. Forever the soul remains there and with no aging, diseases, birth or death. There is happiness, bliss and enjoyment all the time

10

Episode 9- Path to hidden treasure!

Aarj- If you think this knowledge is so divine, scientific and so true then why does not everyone know about it? I never heard or read this in my school or college as well. This is not mentioned in any course books? Where are you getting it all from?

Kris (smilingly)- yeah, that's a secret but I will tell you. I am getting it from some very thousands of years old books. It's like a path to treasure mapped on a piece of paper that goes way back in history. You must have heard about stories of people finding age old gold, gems and other precious stones hidden underground. Some person has probably put together a map on how to find it and it was revealed hundreds of years later. Just because it's not a part of course book, does not mean that it's not true or scientific. Everything I say can be explained with proper science and with factual analysis.

Treasure hunt!

Aarj- ok, I try to understand this but usually people with treasure map don't want to share as they would want to keep all treasure for themselves. But this piece of info that you are sharing does not look like it will deprive others so why would anyone not want to share the knowledge/information?

Kris- Because the Guru of this teaching or knowledge or information has put in very clearly that treat this as "Royal

Secret". It's very high form of knowledge and how royal families keep high level of nation's secrets, similarly this information should be considered as part of intelligence secret. It can be shared only amongst most trustworthy and intelligent people. It's not meant for general public. Share it with only one who has that faith, understanding and who is ready to listen with full dedication.

Even a student need to possess certain qualifications to receive this knowledge. First and foremost, the student should be away from ego, self-obsession and jealousy. A person should be humble enough as this can't be proved or seen with our limited senses of eyes, ears etc. or even with our limited intelligence level.

Another important point that I would like to make here is that wherever your inclination is, you tend to go to that direction and may also get benefits from there. For e.g. if a person needs money or good health or fortune and if he worships respective God or demi god (as per their religious beliefs), he may get it. But what after that? The circle of rebirth will not end and may be in next birth he will need money again and he may again worship the money God. Point I am making is that there is no end to it. End can be achieved by having faith in the highest energy and trying to go to that planet from where no one returns back. This is possible!

Not everyone can understand this and this is why it's said that we should share this fact only with one who is willing to understand. Else, for most of the people, it's beyond their intelligence and a waste of time for people like you and me who are trying to make them understand. It may be very difficult for one to comprehend how the entire nature is created, dissolved and re-created. The cycle will take 4.3 billion years but it has happened over thousands of times, again and again. For another 4.3 billion years, there will be no life on the planet and then slowly the life emerges, various creatures evolve and earth undergoes changes which we are observing now. Again, why you have taken birth as Aarj and me as Kris etc. depends upon the desires we carried when we were leaving our bodies in our last birth. Many friends of yours or even you may not believe in re-incarnation but think logically and scientifically – it does make sense. What is the reason of one being born as rich, handsome and blessed with good fortune while the other who took birth around the same time is ridden with poverty, diseases and ill luck! It's not by chance. There is a mechanism behind it. We are too raw to understand it or may be too materialistic and selfish at times and ignore as we are busy filling up our pockets.

One just has to be very simple and dedicated to get understanding of this **5,000-year-old** knowledge. No gala shows are needed, no pompous celebration required. If one does offer only a leaf, a flower or water with pure love, the blessings of super personality will shower and that would definitely help create interest and understanding of this royal knowledge.

11

Episode 10- Royal Secret

Narration- Aarj now wants to know who all know about this secret. Kris named this knowledge as "Royal Secret".

Aarj- Kris, I want to know more about this secret which you call as "Top notch royal secret".

World is full of intelligent people, rich people who have access to the best libraries or books or some mystics who are trying to understand the working behind this universe in their own way. There may be yogis who spend days and months in meditation or knowers of some other occult sciences.

But you say even they don't possess this information. What's so different about it?

Kris- My dear Aarj, people grasp this information when a knower tells them or if they themselves have a deep desire to know. Like how eye can see everything but it cannot see itself or the tongue can taste everything but it does not know its own taste. Similarly, people may have limited knowledge or limited intelligence to comprehend it. They need to have a genuine teacher or a guide who can explain them. Else it's very difficult for one to understand.

Secret of Royal people

Have a genuine teacher and have faith if you really want to know it. Sometimes we may find a genuine teacher but the student may not be inclined or vice versa. One can't be forced to learn it. So more than 90% of the world population can be ruled out as either they are not interested or they may not have trust in the info I am giving. There may be few % who may be interested from remaining 10% but they may not get the opportunity or the right teacher to learn. So, it does take a bit of destiny as well.

***Aarj*-** ok, I understand and this is why you call it as a secret? Because a very small % of population on the earth may understand this really?

***Kris*-** Yes, Aarj you got it.

Aarj – On another note, you mentioned about that super energetic hero kind of person. What does he know?

***Kris*-** This super energetic person knows everything. Infact he/she is the origin of everything. Or the cause of everything in this universe or all the universes for that matter. But there is no beginning or middle or end in the life of this person. You can take him/her to be like mind amongst all organs of the body or like an ocean amongst all water bodies or letter A of all the alphabets and many more examples can be given. There is no limit on the powers or limit on the magnitude. He/She is the hero of all super heroes. This super energetic is the endless time. Our life span is not more than a dot on this time scale which is running for billions or zillions of years. So, imagine how vast and powerful this person's virtues or energies are. In simple words, it is the seed from which the entire creation has taken place. By creation I don't mean just our planet or our solar system or our galaxy...Creation words includes all galaxies, multiverses, zillions of planets, clusters, gas bodies and everything which is there.

Kris is also giving a genealogical synopsis of the universal population from super energetic person, came out another twenty five powerful great personalities who were given the task of creating innumerable universes, planets and then managing life on those. Life is full of millions of different varieties of species. We are just not talking about the earth but hundreds or thousands of more planets like earth where there could be life.

Narration- Aarj is awestruck at the description of "super-energetic" person. He is wondering how can one be like that. He is lost in his thoughts trying to imagine but this seems again like a fiction or an unimaginable character from some story.

12

Episode 11- Experiencing super power through virtual reality lenses

Aarj- Kris, although I believe every word of what you have just said but can't hold my desire to see this super person. I am thankful to you for providing so intricate and deep details. It seems to me that this person will be out of the world, possessing some super powers that we can't even think of, in control of the best technology to keep the system running beautifully for our nature. I am eager to know more about it and also want to see what its appearance may be like.

Will it be possible for you to show me this person's form or quality or powers? I may be able to understand and perceive all that. Or you don't want to show me assuming am too of an ordinary dumb person to understand that kind of super computer?

Kris-This sight could be most exciting at the same could be most horrifying for you. You must have never see so various colors, shapes and powers together. You could not even imagine what that would be like. It will be so bright as if hundreds of suns are shining together. It's just not possible to see that with our bare-naked eyes. I will have to provide you with special eye lenses embedded in a high-tech VR set so you could see that but even with that you won't be able to hold for more than few seconds.

I am again warning you – it may raise your heart beat, make your hair stand in fear and ecstasy at the same time. You need to be mentally prepared enough to be able to handle that kind of stimulation.

Aarj- After hearing this, I am more excited to know all about that power and somehow also get a glimpse of what it is like. Please show it to me. I feel I can take it and I am mentally prepared.

Kris- ok, if you insist so. I will give you the gadget that you need to wear all the time while we are watching this "super" hero. Else it may cause irreparable damage to your eyes.

Narration – with that Kris took out a special gadget and asked Aarj to wear it around his head. Thousands of people are gathered in the stadium but they won't be able to perceive any of this because they are not wearing those hi-tech lenses. In fact, they have no idea what Kris and Aarj are even talking about. Still few minutes remain before the boxing game starts but now Aarj is not worried about game, he is eager to see this "super-energetic" hero. If you remember, Sam is also narrating all this to Duro's father. Kris is fully aware that Sam's cameras have been recording every conversation and also capturing videos. Kris does not stop those cameras from working although he could have easily deactivated them. He is fine with Sam and Duro's father watching all of it. Actually, secretly he may want them to. Why? We may find an answer later.

Finally, Aarj was ready with his super powerful lenses and Kris is now ready to press the "on" button. Within seconds on starting, Aarj heard thundering and terrible sounds with smoke, fire and heat all over. Clouds of smoke are still there but Aarj with the help of his special vision, was now able to see through the clouds and the deeper he sees, the most unbelievable sight comes up. Aarj is feeling very warm on one side of the body and freezing on the other side!

Aarj- Kris, what is all this? I can't believe what I am seeing. I see many mouths, many eyes, many ears decked with powerful and precious gems, most dangerous weapons, many arms and also there are many faces all the sides. It's so bright and shining as if thousands of suns are shining together, throwing their brilliance.

I can see the entire universe, our planet and thousands of more planets with lives on them. I can also see earth and exactly the place where we all are seated and I see Aarj and Kris there talking with each other. I see the past, present and I can also see future that I am living a peaceful affluent life with my family and friends. This is so incredible. I am seeing innumerable forms extended all sides. I see everything in there, innumerable planets and celestial bodies, mountains, rivers, oceans, fire, sky, all other gods and demi gods, blazing fire which is hard to gaze at even with this gadget.

Scary , exciting, spine chilling- Aarj pleading to stop this!

I even see hundreds of dangerous and poisonous animals. There does not seem to be a beginning, middle or end of this form. Is this what we call infinity? I see sun and moon as the eyes, blazing fire from this person's mouth and the radiance is maintaining this universe. I am not able to look as my eyes can't take this brilliance. I am also horrified looking at all this stupendous and dreadful form.

I feel I have lost my self-control and peace and I am quite frightened seeing these blazing eyes, mouth wide open where continuously creatures are going in and coming out.

I even see my uncles, aunts, even Duro and his brothers. I see the boxing game is taking place. I see that I have started winning the game and everyone is cheering me up. What is all this? Is this real future or am I dreaming?

I am bewildered, horrified and can't find any peace so please do me a favor, stop showing me this and please take me back to the normal world.

Narration- Kris changes the settings of virtual reality glasses and ask Aarj to close his eyes for few seconds. When Aarj opens his eyes, he does not see that terrible frightening form but he sees a strong, calm and serene super hero standing with a bliss and smile on his face.

Aarj- This form has been changed and I feel so happy and at peace after seeing this calm form of the super energetic person.

Kris- Yes, this form is very relaxing and this super hero can take you to the best planet ever where everyone lives in happiness all the time.

Narration – with that, Kris takes away the gadget and special lens. Aarj is almost unconscious and he takes few minutes to open his eyes with his head spinning. He looks around to see that Kris is sitting next to him, ring is getting ready, his brothers are smiling and are happy and he sees Duro with angry red eyes staring at him from the other side. Everything seems to be normal. His heart beat and pulse is getting normal and he looks at Kris. Kris as always is smiling at him and encouraging him to get ready for the game.

Aarj- Kris, which world did you take me to? I still feel my hair standing at the end and I don't know if all what I saw was true or was I dreaming?

Kris- It was not a dream. You saw the "super-energetic" hero who is the creator, maintainer and even the destroyer of this universe. You saw the future as well. Things are bound to happen and all human beings are just instruments in the hands of the controller. We are like puppets so we need to worry less and work more. You should do what is expected out of you and don't worry what would happen next. You are very fortunate to have experience this sight. No one else has got that opportunity so far. Even the best of best would like to see this but they may not get a chance. You had it, you saw how the world is being controlled, please understand this knowledge, analyze it and do what is expected of you. Don't sit and weep like a child. You have to go and fight, regardless of the outcome of the game. This is not the time to step back. History will laugh at you and so would people and they won't hesitate to call you a coward. Will you be ok with such a title?

What you have experienced now may not be perceived by so called richest people, scholars of the world or highly accomplished intellectuals. Even after spending ten years in Universities, you may not be able to understand how the world is functioning, who is behind all this and how we are actually only instruments in the hands of the nature. People may spend their lives learning and reading or performing rituals or austerities, still they would not be lucky enough to see what you did.

Narration – Aarj doubts are slowly going away and his mind is becoming clear. He is regaining his confidence and gradually looks like is ready to get into the ring with a clear heart and mind. This is how a sports person should be.

13

Episode 12- What does this Super Hero like? Can he help Aarj?

———♡———

Narration- There are still few minutes left for the boxing game to begin. Aarj takes that opportunity and again asks a question. He is more curious now. He does not think if his questions are considered to be dumb or intelligent but he does not want to bury the curiosity. So here he goes again....and very patiently Kris will reply back.

Aarj- Kris, after seeing this super energetic hero, I am sure that there is a controller behind everything that is happening – in material form or in spiritual form or in nature or in this universe or beyond. I feel we all are so trivial and absolutely under the control of the super energy. I understand that in our previous conversation you were trying to share this information. I could not understand then. But if I got it right, you meant to say that we need to understand what reality is and try to reach to the highest possible planet where people don't age, don't fall sick and away from all sorrows and miseries. You also showed me a simpler human like form and asked to get powers from him. At the same time, you mentioned that one can also be fully devoted in one's thoughts and one's actions. So, what is the better way of connecting oneself with super energetic in order to be able to port ourselves to top most place? Will it be meditating or thinking continuously about the super hero or should we follow some special ritual or should we completely surrender? What should one do? What kind of people can be ported to the super hi-fi most advanced planet?

Kris- Its said that those who fix their mind in being devoted to super energetic form and are mentally and emotionally always engaged even while doing their day to day jobs, are considered to be most perfect candidate who could be taken to the highest planet.

There are people those who would like to be more knowledge focused, meditate, contemplate and control senses, live a strict life and equal to all will also come to the highest planet but this path is difficult, need more work and it also takes time. Easier way is to just be devoid of ego and surrender oneself with the thought that doer is someone else and I am just the instrument in the hands of the controller. This is much simpler and quick way to do. The other alternate way will also ultimately take to the same point but it takes more time and more effort and mind may not always support as it involves lot of sacrifice and austerities.

If the elevator is available, why does one want to climb stair cases to reach on 30th floor. If the person does not stop climbing, he will eventually reach the top floor but look at the effort and pain one has to take.

Why take stairs when there is an elevator?

Another point that I would like to make here is that super energetic says those who follow the path of devotion need not worry about reaching the goal as the super energy itself comes to take them to higher planet and they get away from the pains of birth, death and re birth. So, the responsibility to port the soul to higher planets lie with the ultimate controller and not with ourselves. This is definitely less taxing and more relaxing. There is not even any need to spend hundreds of hours reading, analyzing, discussion, intellectual conferences. none of that is required. Its good if one wants to do all that kind of intellectual contemplation/ speculation while one is still devoted and full of faith. Gathering intellectual information surely does not hurt, moreover it is anyways enhancing our knowledge. But just by itself it may not be possible for us to understand. One needs a very learned and spiritual guru/teacher who can make sure we stay on the path without being deviated.

So, again I would like to say that just fix your mind on the devotional joyful form and think about super energetic hero all the time and fall in love with that form.

But if you think, that's not possible then let's follow the simple devotional rules like read your mantras/prayers, purify your senses, follow the rituals etc.

If you think even following devotional rules is not possible, then try to offer all the work you do to the supreme. Have a feeling that you are working for the controller of the creation.

And last, if one can't even work in that kind of consciousness, then just give up all the results of your work and be happy in self.

So, there are various stages given and in the most simplified ways.

It may not be still easy and if we one can't follow the path of surrender, then cultivate knowledge. From knowledge, raise yourself up to meditation. From meditation, again elevate yourself up to the level to the extent when you are ready for renunciation of your fruits of action- at least mentally. By such kind of mental renunciation, one can attain peace of mind.

Renunciation does not mean withdrawing oneself from regular day to day activities or ignore our goals and sit in a lethargic way all day. Aarj was one of the best boxer and still he practiced 8-10 hours a day!! He will also fight vigorously against his component but even after doing his best, he may still lose the game. Or may-be he will win. Outcome can be either victory or defeat but let's not feel attached to the outcome. As all we can control, are our efforts not the end results. After being extremely honest with our own efforts, even if we lose the game, we should not get upset and rather embrace the defeat as we would have embraced victory. Let's accept the results, analyze what went wrong, work on our weaknesses and be ready again with more zeal and enthusiasm. If in this process, any time you feel there has been any injustice against you, then you should definitely raise your voice and be not scared of unveiling the truth.

Aarj- Ok, I am trying to understand the various ways of reaching to the highest place but tell me one thing what kind of people are most dear to supreme or super energetic? Share some qualities so I can assess for myself? As super hero would be inclined to help those ones first.

Kris- Let me tell you what kind of person is always loved by Super hero. Someone who is never envious, who is friend to all living entities – including animals and plants, who does not carry false ego, who is equal in both happiness and distress and who always is contented inside, full of gratitude and is engaged in the thoughts of going to highest planet, is very dear to the Super energetic. One other quality you can see is usually this kind of person is very calm, quiet, patient, does not get disturbed in any circumstances. He/She always remains joyful. He has just surrendered himself but that does not mean that he is lazy and not working hard or not putting his best efforts. He is doing all of that but with a calm mind as he knows that his job is not be worried about results but his job is to just put in his best efforts.

This person is not in anxiety or stress and neither he gives anxiety, sorrow or stress to anyone else. Such a person is full of compassion and kindness for all. Cleanliness of both body and soul is important to him. His house may be simple but would be clean and away from clutter. Loss and gains of money or property keep happening in our lives but one who does not get very happy nor anxious is the one who is considered to carry those virtues.

This person understands that honor and dishonor are again part of material lives and two sides of a coin. They don't get disturbed or very proud of their accomplishments as they know that it's all temporary. He may speak less but that does not mean that one should not speak, it means that one should not speak unnecessarily or one should not speak nonsense. Some people have the habit of blabbering just to attract other's attention. They look like fools in the eyes of intelligent people.

With this, I have tried to explain lot of the qualities and habits of a person who will be liked by super hero. Analyze yourself Aarj and see if you belong there.

Narration – Aarj basically wanted to test himself if he can be promoted to higher planets but he could not ask directly to Kris as he was afraid of being told that he does not belong to that category. So, he is asking question indirectly – he wants to know what does that ideal person do, think or live. Kris understood that very well and thus in the end he says that analyze yourself and see where you are in this journey.

14

Episode 13- What are 24 elements which make up everything we see or feel!

Narration- Do you really think Aarj questions will stop here? He is more inquisitive about the knowledge and now he is thinking of how the body is different than soul and the super soul or super energetic?

Aarj- Kris, I am not fully satisfied with the information you gave me so far. Tell me more facts, which layman are not aware of. Would like to know how wise people should treat body and the soul? I have heard many people saying that there is no distinction between the energy that we have within ourselves and the super energetic one. Tell me more about the nature and I have heard things about "field" but have no idea what this is all about.

Kris- Aarj, I will tell you all about it. First of all, lets understand what is nature, who is the enjoyer of the nature, what is field, who are the knowers of the field and what kind of knowledge do they possess. Let me again explain in very simple words how the world works. We have something called "soul" inside us which never dies. Our body may die – e.g. Aarj may die but Aarj's consciousness inside does not die and it goes out of the dead body and starts looking for some other body. Can Aarj's consciousness/power/soul say that – oh give me body of Mr. World? I want that. There are many others who would that so how does it work? First come, first serve? Or stand in queue and wait for your turn? Or maybe make a reservation online! ;)

No, at the time when soul is leaving the body, that decayed body may have some unfulfilled desires and it died with those desires. And at the same time an account is maintained of all good and bad deeds of that body. Based on the desires and based on his karma, the soul gets a suitable body which may enable it to fulfill the unfulfilled desires of last birth. E.g. a dying body might have a very deep desire to be a successful business man and maybe he was not able to get there. In the next birth, he may have some natural inclination towards doing business or being an entrepreneur or as we discussed earlier, someone could have been too attached to his/her dog and he may also get body of a dog in next birth if his desires were too strong.

So, what we do with this body determines the next outcome. This all is done in the middle of material nature, which is "nature" here.

All the activities are happening in the body and thus it is called "field"- field of actions!

The one who is knowledgeable enough to understand this field is called "knower of the field". This knower of the field could not be anyone but our inner consciousness or the spark that we have which makes this body living or it is the soul in other words. So first of all, not every soul can be knower of the field but even if it becomes one, it can know only about its own field meaning its own body and the actions body is performing. "Knower of the field" could be the one who has stopped identifying himself/herself to the body as it knows that body is different from true self.

There is something called "Super soul" which is even superior to "soul" as that super soul or super energetic is the knower of ALL the fields. A very good example can be given is of painter, painting and easel! See what fits in which role here.

Summarizing, conditioned soul (knower of the field) gets a body (field) to work towards fulfillment of old desires. Body is made of senses so it's natural to see body working towards satisfaction of senses but the inner soul knows what is permanent and what is temporary and useless.

So, let me tell you what this world consists of. It is a very old and deep science knowledge which probably today's science is yet to validate. It has not yet reached to that high level.

Body or field of activity consist of twenty four elements.
-

Everything in this world is made up of five most important elements which are – air, earth, water, fire and ether. (5 no.)

There are three other subtle elements in human being which are false ego, intelligence and modes of nature. (3 nos.) Modes of nature can again be divided into good, passion or bad.

Then there are five senses which are needed to acquire knowledge. These are eyes, ears, nose, tongue and touch. (5 no.)

Again, there are five more organs which are needed to work – Voice, arms, legs, anus and genital. They are needed to have a smooth functioning of the body. (5 no.)

One of the most important sense which is on top of all the ones mentioned is – "Mind"! (1 no.)

Lastly there are five objects of senses – Smell, taste, warmth, touch and sound (5 no.)

So, adding up all the above, it comes to twenty-four elements of body or field. Now let me tell you that body also goes through six different stages –

Birth, grows, stays, produces, decays and vanishes!

Let me give you one more piece of information from a different angle. When five sense elements in the body interact, they lead to desires, hatred, pleasure and pain. So, you see pain and pleasure has nothing to do with soul. It's all limited to gross body which is not going to last for long.

Thus, the ultimate enjoyer (super energetic) designed the material nature which is made up of twenty-four elements. It has given us a field and also a knower of the field if we can develop that knowledge and if we can see a difference between our body and our soul. On top of everything is super–soul which is knower of all the fields in the world. Our soul has all the qualities of super soul but it's not the same. E.g. sun and sun rays are different although their characteristics are same. The essence of this knowledge is that knower is permanent but field is temporary and is a facility given to us to be able to see the reality and truth. Unfortunately, only one in millions may be interested and one in those thousands may actually question like you and one in those hundreds may be able to really follow and live the life accordingly. Only those ones go to the highest planet and others just keep migrating from one body to the other. There are 8.4 million different bodies and you may get one based upon your nature, desires and actions!

One who understands the above knowledge, naturally becomes non-violent, very patient and compassionate in nature. The advancement on this path happens gradually but it's essential to maintain cleanliness – both external and internal and persistence. By this we can understand the relationship between our soul and the super soul or our energy and the super energy!

A comparison cannot be made between individual soul and super soul as super soul has only spiritual senses. An individual soul can also have spiritual senses once we clean up the dust of material senses which is accumulated on the soul. This is what the knowledge does. Trying to clean up the dust and show the true picture in the mirror!

Summarizing, anyone who can see three things – the body, the proprietor of the body or individual soul and the friend of the individual soul is really knowledge!

15

Episode 14- Three modes and a castle with nine gates

Narration – Arjun was quiet and contemplating. Seems his questions were coming to an end but Kris did not want to stop here. He himself started telling Aarj that there are few more pieces of information he would like to share.

Kris- I am so glad you took interest so far as this discussion could turn out to be boring for most of the people as they are not blessed enough to understand this. Their lives go away in managing their day to day desires, ambitions and accumulating wealth or just enjoying and sleeping. I know you are not asking me anything further but I feel since we have come so far, I should disclose couple more pieces here. Have you heard about modes of natures?

Aarj- Thanks Kris. I am just trying to absorb all what you have told me and shown me. Regardless, I am very much interested in knowing more from you. No, I don't know the modes of nature. Kindly explain me what those are.

Kris- I will tell you all about modes of natures. We all take birth with certain inherent nature. There can be three different qualities of that nature –it can be in goodness, passion and ignorance. But that does not mean that we restrict ourselves to one of these modes throughout our lives. It keeps changing. In fact, we keep jumping into passion from goodness or from ignorance and vice versa. We have many different emotions in a single day which means we will act under the influence of different modes. There is a science behind this also. Why do certain people act under certain modes?

We as human beings are influenced or bound to different nature but the super- energetic is beyond these natures. And if we port ourselves to the best planet, we can also come out of it.

Currently, our thinking and actions are influenced by these qualities/inherent nature and if we can act or think without getting contaminated – that would mean we have really attained the highest knowledge.

People say life comes out of matter but is that really true? Let's keep matter next to each other or lets mix them up but still life could not be generated out of it. Life is a combination of material matter and spiritual matter. E.g. the scorpion lays its eggs in piles of rice but it cannot be said that scorpion is born out of rice.

And based on our past life activities and desires, we get a body in the current birth and we sometimes enjoy or sometimes suffer in this body. Because we get different kinds of bodies and different natures which comes with the body, one is induced to act accordingly to that nature. Dog will act like dog only and so would a pig.

Three inherent qualities possessed by all

Now let me explain the three modes. Let's go one by one.

<u>Mode of Goodness</u>- one who has a sense of advancement in material knowledge, wiser than most of the people, has a sense of happiness as he is not effected much by our day to day life miseries. This person does not have thoughts of harming others and is mostly contented in his life. There is a problem to this as well. This person believes that he is better than others and just by this thinking he develops a

sense of pride or ego of goodness. This kind of feeling will not let the person go to higher planet. So even by being in mode of goodness, we can be stuck.

Now let me tell you about <u>Mode of Passion-</u>

These kinds of people are very hard working, ambitious, full of energy and full of desires. They want to have honor in the society, wants to have a happy family, caring and obedient children, good spouse, luxurious house, cars and a good bank balance. In order to achieve all this, one has to work hard every day. Most of this world is in mode of passion these days. It's very difficult for these kinds of people to travel to higher planets. If people in mode of goodness can't reach there, then it's almost impossible for one who is living into passion. There is always a sense of achieving more, get on the higher position, aim for bigger income and house and so on. Contentment is on the lower side and ambitions keep driving person all throughout his life. Person works very hard and toil like a donkey all life to satisfy his senses. They keep forgetting that this all cannot go back with them when they take up a new body.

Now the third one is called – <u>Mode of ignorance</u>

This is just opposite of mode of goodness and it puts the person under delusion. It leads to madness (doing or saying things which don't make sense to a reasonable person), over sleeping, over eating and lazing around. They are not knowledgeable like the first category- they don't know the science behind higher and lower planets, taking re birth based on one's actions, thoughts and desires, they would not like to make any advancement spiritually. They are not even as active as person in the second category which is passion. They don't like to work hard and in fact would like to sleep for 10-12 hours a day, they may be addicted to intoxicants and would not even feel shy of making fun of those into mode of goodness.

So, Aarj let me summarize it for you. We saw three different categories of people those who live in three different modes. First mode, goodness will take one to happiness and contentment, second mode of passion will give them fruits of action and third mode of ignorance will just lead them to become lazy and insensible or mad at times.

Thus, when one dies in goodness, he is definitely taken to higher and better planets, passion stays on earth only and the one in ignorance is taken to lower planets where there is more pain and suffering. Lower planet could mean animal kingdom. They may come back as a dog or cat or even a lion but end of the day, it's an animal which has limited and lower intelligence. So, we may again miss a chance to understand the real knowledge as it's not possible to grasp that in the body of an animal.

But in this age, it's very difficult for one to live 100% in one single mode. We keep getting into different modes based upon the situations or our own mental conditioning. Even in a single day we may switch from goodness to passion to ignorance. They keep competing amongst themselves. By default, most of the people are attracted to second or third mode. It takes practice, guidance, sacrifice and persistence to stay in the first mode. But it's doable if one has full faith in the process which is laid out for it.

Aarj- But how does one know if he/she is in the first mode of goodness?

Kris- Excellent question! Again, there is a science behind it. Let me tell you about nine gates. Do you know what they are? These are the nine holes or gates in our body- two eyes, two ears, two nostrils, the mouth, genital and anus. All these nine gates should be in harmony with each other and function in goodness. E.g. one should be able to see or hear things in right position, taste food which is pure and good...one becomes cleansed inside and outside and every gate develops the symptoms of happiness and that's how you can evaluate if you are fully in goodness.

Animal killing is done by people who live in ignorance. One of the grossest kind of ignorance is to kill animals for the taste of the tongue. They are not aware and it will lead them to darkness eventually.

Nutshell – goodness leads to purity, passion will definitely bring stress and anxiety with material success factors and ignorance is simply foolishness. By no means, I say that one should not work hard. Even if you are in passion and would like to amass great wealth, name and fame... it's fine as long as you are using it for the benefit of entire human kind and not just for yourselves. This is how one's money and wealth can become pure even though it was acquired in the mode of passion.

So now you know three modes, evaluate yourselves and book a ride to either higher planets or lower or stay at the same place. Choice is ours. This is the law of nature and there is no involvement or tempering of anyone else.

16

Episode 15- Huge upside down Banyan tree

Now for a change, before Aarj could ask any further question, Kris himself continued –

"Aarj, imagine this world to be like a huge banyan tree. One who is entangled in this material world would keep on jumping from one branch to the other and there is no end to it. The roots are growing upwards or lets put in a way that the roots are coming down on earth from the top most higher planet. Roots are upwards and branches are downwards. Where can one find this kind of tree? It's simple, we can see it everywhere around us... We just have to see its reflection in the lake or river. This means what we see in this world is a reflection of the real spiritual tree. Reflection turns into material one which is full of desires. Reflection can be temporary- meaning sometimes it can be seen, sometimes it can't be seen. But the origin is always there.

Reflection of upside down tree

Let's imagine again – big huge tree with its branches spread in all the directions. Human beings, animals, other living creatures situated on lower part of the branches and upper part is the hope for higher level of creatures such as demigods, fairies, angels etc. This tree is nourished by three modes of material nature which we just spoke about. Twigs of the tree are sense objects which we enjoy through our senses of touch, hear, smell etc. There is no end to this tree.

Its huge and very dense. One keeps getting stuck into it as if it was a maze, but if we can come out of it, we see the light of higher planet, a life full of bliss and only happiness. For that we need to keep making way through each and every branch and try to reach to the higher level where we see the light. It's going to be dark below.

How can one make its way through the dense branches now? It can be done by this knowledge that the world is temporary and we need to go to the higher planets so we can be away from life of misery and sorrow. I am not saying there is no happiness on earth but it's not consistent. That highest planet does not even need the light of sun or moon to illumine itself. It has its own light or self-luminous. One who goes there does not ever need to come back down to lower planet of earth. One can go only with this knowledge and no aircraft or rocket can take the person there.

Previously we talked about the super energetic person. Actually, we all are part of that super energetic person, we have those qualities but they are at very minute level. But let me tell you there are two kinds of living creatures even with those qualities. First are those who live on this planet earth and second category is that who live on higher planet. Let me tell you the difference between these two. First one is like us- we take birth, we grow, we get old and we die. On the higher planet, living beings don't go through this cycle. No one dies there, no one gets old there, no one even falls sick. Imagine what kind of world it would be.

Again, this is the knowledge people are not aware about. People keep speculating on what all planets are there in this universe or multiverse and what happens there but we all keep ourselves busy in discussions which may not be very fruitful. Rather than these pseudo intellectual speculations, if one just puts some trust in this old age knowledge, tries to follow and understands with full devotion is actually utilizing his/her limited time on the Earth in real sense.

Time is limited for all, clock keeps ticking. One who utilizes it can get himself out of these clutches soon as compared to others who can spend another thousand years migrating from one body to the another and keep living with less intelligence.

17

Episode 16-Divine or demoniac

Narration- It's not clear if Aarj understood all what Kris mentioned about the tree and its branches. But now he wants to know the qualities of good and bad natured people so he can relate himself and others to those qualities and do a self-evaluation.

Aarj- Tell me Kris what are the qualities of those people whom you call divine or demoniac.

Kris- It's not that hard to possess good qualities. I will name the few to start with. Some basic that we can start with our <u>cleanliness</u> – outside cleanliness is also very important. Have a good hygiene and clean your body thoroughly. It may sound that I am talking about things at gross level but this is the first step. Then we talk about cleaning our hearts and mind. That means, let not the thoughts of jealously, greed and lust enter our mind. Be truthful, try to see how you can elevate yourself to higher planets by going for the real knowledge, be gentle, be noble, and be courteous and make use good use of your words. ANGER is the biggest enemy. Whatever happens try not to let anger influence your body and mind as it does more harm to our body and soul than to the other person.

Who is demon? Who is divine?

Fault finding in others is also condemned. Do that with yourself but not others unless you are a teacher or parent and you want your student or child to grow and be on right path.

You can also assess yourself and see how far have you understood this knowledge. One of the distinct quality of a person who is spiritual is <u>fearlessness</u>. He is not afraid of anything besides doing wrong. This person knows that everything is designed and preset and there is super energetic up there to take care of him, so why to worry? He is not afraid of being left alone, he does not need a constant support of others. That does not mean that this person is anti-social. It just says that his mind is not disturbed if in life he faces situations against him.

Next virtues are to <u>humility</u> and <u>charity</u>. They go hand in hand. More charity you give, should make you more humble and noble but we always see the other way happening in the world. People do charity to puff up their egos and their importance. Those kinds of charity have no meaning as its done with a selfish interest. Also, one very important point is to perform charity is to the right person, at the right place and in right situation. Do not just go with emotions. Your hard-earned money has to be put to good use. Perform charity with presence of mind and once done, don't worry about how your money is put to use. Do not keep fretting on it. Just move on and donate more.

Next thing we will talk about is <u>sacrifice</u>. Do not be shy of making sacrifices in life for the sake of your family, friends or even society. Let me tell you an interesting way our society and lives of people were structured some hundreds of years back. It may not be practical now but mentally we can still do it. In our thousands of years old scriptures, it is said that a person should divide his life into four different parts. Let's say life of a person is one hundred years then first twenty-fve years should be spent on studying, gaining knowledge and being a student. Next twenty-five years should be focused on building family – like getting married, having children, their upbringing, other social and family commitments, charity, saving money etc. Next twenty-five years one should spend in forest. Well it's not possible now but what it means is now in this phase one should stop thinking about money all the time and be detached with the material possessions and have a retired life. Retired life does not mean being lazy. It means having a disciplined life and giving back to the society in whatever ways possible and also gaining our own spiritual knowledge so we can get back on the higher planet. Plan for that journey. In today's context, we can take forest to be a quiet, peaceful life and may be move to a small town or village. Most of the people find peace that way.

Next and last twenty-five years should be spent in renunciation. Again, it's not possible to leave everything and carry two sets of clothes and go and sit under a tree for meditation. But we can achieve it in our mind. In this phase of life, our mind should be completely detached. Children have grown up- they can take care of themselves and their offspring, we can spend time in self-realization and may be reading more of our valuable scriptures and just understand what this life is all about. Also spread this knowledge. Do not take unnecessary work on your shoulders as this phase is just meant for focusing on the super energetic, trying to self-analyze, develop more virtues to make sure we are on our journey to higher planet.

We have discussed there are total of sixteen good qualities – let me put them again –fearlessness, purification – internal and external, gaining true knowledge, humility, charity, sacrifice, self-study, nonviolence, truthful, away from anger, cleanliness, hearing from our seniors, not find fault in others, not being frustrated or agitated, self-control and freedom from jealousy.

Now let me talk about demoniac qualities – arrogance, pride, anger, conceit, harshness and ignorance. This is a royal road to self-destruction.

The demoniacs are engaged in activities that will lead the world to the destruction. These people are more violent and they become crueler to plants, animals and to human beings. Animal killing is very prominent amongst these people. These people are considered the enemies of the world as ultimately, they will invent or create something which will definitely destroy or contaminate the entire world. Weapons of mass destruction, viruses causing pandemics and can be deadly. They are always busy in hoarding wealth or engaging themselves in sense pleasures. They may even get false honor in the world but the truth is that they are on the road to destruction, even though they may consider themselves to be very smart.

These people do not believe in law of karma. Up to the last day of their life they work only to gratify their senses, not realizing that this is a never-ending loop. They die, take birth and again get into the clutches of satisfying desires. The wheel goes on. This person does not believe in the super natural power but thinks he only is the doer and he can create or destroy things with his material wealth, accumulate power, riches etc. This person may perform charities but that is only for the sake of the name. These kinds of people are usually bewildered by false ego, strength, pride, lust and anger and do not understand that the present life is the preparation for the next life. The prominent qualities of a demoniac person are typically three – **lust, anger and greed.** Stay away from these to the extent possible as they can be very dangerous. It says that one should rely on this **5,000-year-old** knowledge from the scriptures as otherwise the conditioned/material person is prone to following four defects –

a. Imperfect senses – we are not able to see or understand the truth with these senses

b. Propensity to cheat – all human beings have it in order to gain material wealth or power

c. Committing mistakes – we always do as human beings-to err is human

d. Illusion – since our senses are imperfect, we are under illusion, most of the times.

Thus, here I have explained the people with divine and demoniac qualities. I hope you know now what to be careful of.

18

Chapter 17 - Everything in the world fits into three divisions

As expected, Aarj is ready with his next question.

Aarj-Hey Kris, I understand the good and the evil qualities that you explained above and also that how super natural person is so powerful and is the creator of the entire universe. But there are lots of people on this planet who may not believe in this so called super natural person. They may have their own gods, leaders or someone else whom they consider to be a powerful person. So, are they right in their capacity?

Narration – point to note here is that in fourth chapter Kris mentioned that one can have faith in any power and ultimately, they will get the knowledge but in sixteenth chapter he kind of contradicts himself by saying that anyone who does not follow the principles laid down for the benefit of humankind is like a demon himself.

Let's see how Kris clears up the doubt.

Kris- Hey Aarj, I can understand that you may find this bit confusing. Let's go back to our basis. We have discussed earlier that modes of nature can be of three types – goodness, passion or ignorance. Any faith that a person believes in or does not believe in, follows this knowledge or does not- depends upon which modes are influencing his basic nature. As I said earlier this nature comes from previous births and is continuously getting worked upon. It depends upon who are they associated with. A person who is ignorant or lazy can change his nature by making friends with people who are more in the modes of goodness or passion, i.e. hard working.

So again, under the influence of these three modes of nature or any of these three, a person may develop a particular kind of faith or attitude in life. E.g. a person in goodness may try to get deeper into real truth or real knowledge and try to understand why we have taken birth, why some people are rich and some poor, some get fortunate and make millions, while some may lose everything even after being very honest and hard working. There is another power which is ruling all these systems and cycles. These kinds of people who want to understand and know more about these topics can be considered in mode of goodness as they are not driven here by the desire to acquire more wealth, power or recognition. They understand that this <u>birth is rare</u> and is meant to learn the working on the creation.

On another note, people those are influence by mode of passion are very hard working, ambitious, material goal oriented and will work day and night to achieve their goals. They are programmed to be this way because they have been influenced by the association of like-minded people. For them acquiring wealth, recognition, high post and even making huge charity might be the main goal of life. They go through mood swings, sometimes they get very happy upon achieving success and failures may even push them into depression. They lament and feel pain of losing material belongings because they fail to understand the true knowledge, that there is a science behind everything that's happening and that's designed to happen. Their faith may be in some power whom if they worship, it may give them immense wealth or power or fulfill their desire to conquer something in this world. There is nothing wrong in that, one can lead this life too but the pain comes when one does not realize the true mechanism. If one keeps working hard and surrender the results to the super power, one does not feel so much pain or too much happiness as he thinks that his job is to just do the work with full honesty and integrity and rest the person leaves upon the super power.

There are third kind of people – those who are influenced by ignorance. They are usually lazy, like to eat junk food, procrastinate, tell lies and want to acquire money or power but by all wrong means. According to this nature of theirs, they may have faith say in some person who can convince them that through some magic or tricks, he can make it happen and the person can be the owner of huge wealth. These kinds of people may put their faith in so called wizards or magicians or some fake guru.

Different modes

People in mode of goodness may worship their gods, passionate one may worship demi gods or even demons and ones who are ignorant, may want to worship ghosts or spirits.

Like how we heard during world war time that a person was worshipping and thanking Hitler day and night as his business grew more than ten times due to war and he amassed great wealth. Would you like to worship or put your faith in Hitler?

We see some people not eating at all or staying for months without food and water or standing on one feet for hours and hours to please their gods or their faith. This is again not of any use as it may not take the person to the higher planet. We saw that we need to make our journey from earth to other better planets where actually there is life and people don't grow old or don't get sick. These kind of austerities or hardship taken over in order to fulfill one's ego or pride is definitely a sign of ignorance.

But there can be better austerities or duties of cleanliness, simplicity, non-violence or celibacy which lead to goodness of body. Control on our words when we speak is goodness of our tongue and qualities such as serenity, self-control, purity of thought is an austerity of mind which takes us towards modes of goodness.

Similarly, kind of food we eat also is according to the modes of nature and sometimes they may change our mode of nature too. People in goodness would want to eat more nutritious, juicy, natural and healthy meals which may give happiness to body, mind and soul. On the other hand, most of the people these days like to eat food that is very spicy, sour, or too hot or too salty or overly cooked and this kind of food may fulfill the desire of our taste buds but is not good for our body and it may lead to diseases. People in ignorance like to eat all nasty and weird kind of food that is mostly made up by killing animals. They will cause pain not just to themselves but to the entire world and may lead to a pandemic situation.

Again, it's said one should perform charity but charity also gets influenced by our modes. Some people may give donation to real needy and they will not do that in order to gain name and fame. That is real charity which is performed at the right place, out of one's duty and given to right recipient. People who are influenced more by passion also perform huge charities but they have a desire to get something back in return – may be a desire to see people calling them philanthropist or newspapers publishing about them.

People in ignorance may also perform charity but they may not help people who are really needy, they may not do it out of their duty, not being done at the right place. This kind of charity is useless.

One who is above the mode of goodness is the one who just renounces all the actions. Now that is quite difficult path to be on.

One can assess his own nature and evaluate if one's actions take him/her to goodness, passion or sheer ignorance.

Are you now satisfied Aarj? It's almost time now for you to go in the ring and fight for the right cause.

19

Chapter 18- Finally Aarj, now get up and fight

Aarj- Yes, I must go now but if you may allow, can I ask just one last question?

Kris (smilingly) – ok, go ahead

Aarj- it's quite interesting to know how you have classified almost everything on this world into three categories. But in between you mentioned something about "giving up the results" or I guess you used the word "renunciation". What do you actually mean by renunciation? How can I give up my own deeds and not enjoy the fruits of my own action?

Kris- ok, it's a valid question and let me explain you something here.

What do you understand by word sacrifice or renunciation? It does not mean that we should stop doing actions, stop working, stop playing or stop studying and may be go to some secluded cave in order to start meditating. This is not the right meaning here. What this word signifies is to give up the "results" of all the activities. Remember carry on your activities with 100% devotion and honesty but after that don't worry about the results and just leave it on super natural power.

Activities should be carried on as a matter of one's duty. E.g. after you get up in the morning, it's your duty to make your own bed or help in household chores. Whether you get praise for that or not, it should not matter.

Similarly – when we see the needy people in the world, let's do charity and make donations. They purify us internally but it should not be done with the objective of getting recognition and praise. That just defeats the purpose. Also, as I mentioned earlier, charity is effective only when it is given to right people, at right place and in right circumstances. Charity done to unworthy people is not counted towards charity and thus does not get recorded in your good books.

Lot of people in this world perform their task out of passion – e.g. Steve jobs was passionate about his work, this is absolutely fine. If needed one should put in even more than 100% but then leave the task there after doing your best. That again says that do it with the mindset that – "I have done my best and I leave the results on the nature". This way the undesirable results do not bring agony or pain as there is an acceptance already set in our mind. This is the key to lead a happy life.

I told you about three different modes earlier. Do you remember them? Let me tell again, these are goodness, passion and ignorance.

Those who are performing activity by staying in first mode, which is goodness, are happy in all the situations. Whether the work is small or big, they don't get bothered. They don't hate inauspicious work and neither they are quite attached to auspicious activity. The work is done as part of the person's duty.

The gist of all this conversation is that _duties should never be given up._ So, one who does not do his duty is acting in ignorance, one who does as troublesome or out of fear or for the reason of reward, is said to be in passion and one that does happily because it needs to be done is said to be doing that in goodness.

Talking about duties or work, do you know typically there are five different factors that one needs to understand. No work can be done without these <u>five causes</u> or factors.

These are –

1. Place – there has to be a place of performance
2. Worker – person who is performing the work
3. Endeavor – action of performing
4. Five Senses – without these no work can be done
5. Inspiration or super soul power sitting inside us.

I told you this so you understand how an action is taking place. It's a combination of all the above five factors and they need to be in perfect harmony in order to achieve a "good" result.

While performing any action, a doer can get influenced by again the kind of intelligence one has. So, we again divide everything into those three categories. Whether we are talking about knowledge, or any action/karma or the doers- again it all gets divided into three broad categories. By now, I am sure you must be knowing what categories I am referring to.

Let's talk about the <u>three kinds of knowledge</u> –

Knowledge by which one undivided spiritual nature is seen in all existence is said to be in goodness. When we see different type of living entity and miss seeing the oneness of spirituality then it is said to be in passion and where a person is only attached to the result of the activity or action without knowledge of truth is said to be in ignorance.

a. By which oneness in seen in all souls or bodies. They may have different bodies like that of man, beast, plant, animal etc. but that spark or soul inside all of us is same. Everyone carries a spark of that super natural power. This is mode of goodness
b. knowledge by which they see different type of entity dwelling in different bodies is in passion
c. Knowledge by which one is always attached to any kind of work, without knowing full truth is said to be in ignorance or darkness.

By default, all of us fall into third category unless we try to promote ourselves to second or first by deeper understanding.

Similarly, now let's talk about <u>three different kind of action</u> –

Any action in accordance with duty, performed without attachment, without love or hate and by someone who does not care about the fruits of action is said to be in goodness.

Action which is performed with great effort for satisfying one's senses and where person has a sense of false ego, is called action in mode of passion

And any action in ignorance, delusion and which is unethical, injurious is said to be in ignorance.

For example, if you are preparing for your exams and you put in your honest efforts, try to gather notes from all possible sources, read them thoroughly, refer to different text books, get guidance from teachers, fellow students and do hours and hours of practice by burning mid night oil then you are doing the preparation in all good mode and you may pass by flying colors or you may still not! Nevertheless, the action is said to be done in goodness mode.

Other situation, you are doing all the preparation but there is an intense desire for you to top and that does not even stop you from thinking evil. say, you may wish how your closest competitor should fall sick so you can get better marks! Or you may on hide the notes of your friend so he/she does not get to revise the course or any of these kinds of evil thoughts may put us into passion mode. Whether we act on those thoughts or not, still just the presence of them is enough to push us down from goodness to passion.

Third is simple, being ignorant or oblivious of the importance of exams. Just laying around, spending time playing video games or watching you tube, sleeping, not properly planning, not paying attention to notes even when they are right in front of you and then getting late for exams etc. is said to be done in darkness or ignorance. Trying to come up with the ways of cheating in exam to cover up for this laziness. This is called being in ignorance and that's the most pathetic state for any student or for that matter even for a grown up.

Similarly let's talk about <u>three different kind of performers/doers</u> and see what category you fall into, Aarj

Any performer who is aware of the truth of this world and is always happy, enthusiastic and indifferent to success or failure is said to be the person in goodness. Doer who is always attached to the fruits of his action, engaged in satisfying his senses is said to be in passion. And the person who is lazy, procrastinating, obstinate, cheating, insulting others and going against the rules and laws is said to be in ignorance.

Related to these kinds of doers are the three kinds of happiness. One that feels poison in the beginning but ends up like nectar is said to be in goodness. Clear example – say doing crunches or yoga every morning! What a pain to get up early in the morning, half sleepy and then do your Surya Namaskar! But once we are used to it, we start getting happiness by feeling healthy and strong!

And one that feels like lot of pleasure initially and then later ends up in pain is said to be in passion. Eating junk all the time and then suffering from various diseases! Having a milk shake or soda every day is so much fun but months or years down it may bring tremendous pain to our body.

Any happiness which is blind to self- realization, delusion from beginning to end and which arises from sleep, laziness etc. is said to be in ignorance. Lazing around, spending hours on couch browsing channels, not following a proper routine for anything, ignoring hygiene and even health and many more examples could be given.

In none of the planets, there is no one who is not touched by these three modes, right from the superior most planet to earth and to the inferior ones. Even the Angels, witches and demi gods perform action under one of these modes.

In fact, in olden times they divided our society based on the kind of work one does and the mode of nature which influences them. This is also a clear example of dividing society based on our thoughts and action and not based on caste. It's different, that people have started abusing that perfect social system to their advantage. Clearly that was not the intention when the society was divided into four categories. Since we are talking and we have come all the way here, let me quickly tell you about those as well

These four categories are – Intellectuals, rulers or bureaucrats, traders or business owners, and the last and fourth category includes helpers, labors and those who serve others.

Intellectuals are more influenced by goodness as by intellectuals I mean super intellectuals and not just pseudo intellectuals with lots of degrees and certificates. They are meant to teach society how to be tolerant, wise, be friendly and aware towards co-existence, bear right and meaningful knowledge and be peaceful while preaching harmony and wishing welfare for all. Preaching by action and by example and not just by shallow words.

Second section of society includes administrators and rulers and policy makers. They defend the society, nation, be generous to under privileged, possess power, make policies and are very resourceful. They rule the nations under the guidance of the intellectuals who are their trusted advisors.

Third section demonstrate business qualities – they set up big and small business enterprises, enhance trade and commerce, make lot of money and give employment to others. They are also risk takers. They do make money but they believe in putting money to best use as well such as charities to deserving people, making investments in order to spread prosperity in the society, creating more job opportunities so people can earn decent livings and support their families.

Fourth section and last but not least in the order of importance include the section of society whose job is to serve others. They may be streets sweepers, cleaners, helpers and they are meant to serve the other three sections. Lots of people may underestimate their importance but without them the society would not be balanced. They are not highly educated or powerful or resourceful or don't have business acumen but they provide essential services without which the entire system will break. Their importance cannot be underestimated although it's sad to see that they sometimes they don't get a lot of respect or money for the work they perform.

Typically, it's said that first section is influenced by goodness, second and third are more by passion and fourth by ignorance. But one can be above all this if one just does his duty with full faith in the super power and by surrendering the results. If one just does his work with full honesty and commitment and not worry about the results, he will have said to live in perfection. We can just do our best and can't control the outcome so let's learn to accept. Work or prescribed duties should not be renounced but results should be. That kind of person is never lamenting or complaining and is always grateful to Almighty even though he may materially possess almost nothing as compared to others.

Thus, I hope you now understand Aarj that summary of all this discussion again brings us to the point of _performing our duties without expecting fruits of action_. So, get up and get in the ring and start the fight! Your opponent is ready, audience are ready and the show must go on.

Don't feel remorse about hitting your own brother as right now, in this moment, he is more of an opponent than your brother. Play fair, follow rules, don't cheat and don't even carry bad thoughts for him. If he is wrong, he will deserve punishment and does not matter if you give punishment or if nature gives it through you as just one of the instrument.

Aarj- Yes Kris, my entire mind is clear of any doubts. I do feel energized and positive and I know my duty is calling me now. I don't feel weak or guilt any more in my heart and am ready to step into the ring to give one of the best boxing performance of my life. I would like to take 5-10 minutes of quiet time now, contemplating on what an amazing conversation we had, how you showed me the reality through your special lenses and this beautiful and meaningful knowledge that you shared with me. Unfortunately, I never learnt that in school but I do feel how important it is to be aware of spirituality as well, the way we master material sciences.

Narration – With this, Aarj goes back in locker room, gives himself few minutes of quiet time, gets up with a smile and energy, washes his face and walks out with full confidence- the way majestic huge tiger goes out, fully aware of his surroundings but focusing on its prey!

A fierce game

He was ready to fight for his rights, for his brother's rights and to set an example that crying or whining does not get you anything ---situation may go against you but get up and fight and come out of it!

Trumpets, cheer leaders, whistles, applause, clapping, sound, music, lights, cameras ...all are ready! And Aarj looked like a fierce tiger fighting against a mad powerful elephant, very tough game, breath taking, blood shed but finally Duro was knocked down and was too weak to get up at the count of 1- 10 while Aarj was waiting at the neutral white corner.

Victory

Referee counted 1, 2, 3, 4, 5, 6, 7, 8, 9 and the last one 10!!! Whistles, clapping, cheering, party poppers, mobs dancing, some wiping their tears while some jumping around and there stands Kris with a smile at the corner of his lips, slowly clapping his hands while Aarj eyes were searching for him, for his best friend who could guide him when he felt weak and always wished good for him.

Better days waited for them, challenges would come and go but all five brothers always decided to stay on path of goodness, even if that means losing all wealth or possessions that they earned!

Enter Caption

Author has a few professional qualifications and is running a international corporate advisory business. Having spent more than a decade in USA, author has further firmed her believes in old age Indian teachings, Gita shlokas and other valuable treasure of knowledge. Now staying in Hyderabad with her family, is trying to learn more on ancient sanatana values, culture and heritage.

A strong believer in our ancient scriptures, this is a first attempt to translate the Krishna teachings into a light teenage conversational book. She loves reading to her son and other children. Author is a strong believer in vedic astrology and committed to perform any services for benefits of the society while guiding people by way of Jyotish. One has to go through miseries if taken birth on this planet but mankind needs to understand the science behind karmas and make this journey a contented one, even while walking on the path of thorns.

From her birth city, Ujjain to having seen both western and material side of the world, having achieved material success and even earned a reputation of one of the successful entrepreneurs, author is inclined to spend more and more time diving into the ocean of vast ancient knowledge which helps in finding ones true self. This treasure, scientific and logical, is meant to be enjoyed by all. Lets all of us learn together.

Quite enthusiastic towards life, her interest range from philanthropic to start ups, reading Bhagwad Gita to playing golf and guitar. A nature and animal lover by heart is committed to Lord Krishna's teachings.